# The Blemishing of the Potent Child

# The Blemishing of the Potent Child

*Ken Woods*

Writers Club Press
San Jose  New York  Lincoln  Shanghai

The Blemishing of the Potent Child

Writers Club Press
an imprint of iUniverse, Inc.

For information address:
iUniverse, Inc.
5220 S. 16th St., Suite 200
Lincoln, NE 68512
www.iuniverse.com

ISBN: 0-595-19236-X

Printed in the United States of America

To Mary Woods, Arnie Weinmeister and Doug Lent

# Contents

Foreword . . . . . . . . . . . . . . . . . . . . . . . . . . . . . . . . . . . . . . . . . . . . .ix

Introduction . . . . . . . . . . . . . . . . . . . . . . . . . . . . . . . . . . . . . . . . . .xi

Part One: The Blemishing of the Potent Child . . . . . . . . . . . . . . . .1

   1. The Insecurities of King Laius (Lay-es) . . . . . . . . . . . . . . . .5

   2. The Blemishing of Women and the "Sweetheart" Game . . .11

   3. The Invisibility of the Game of Blemish . . . . . . . . . . . . . . .17

   4. Blemish Within the Mental Health Field . . . . . . . . . . . . . .23

   5. The Feelings of Inadequacy and Self-Inflation . . . . . . . . . .27

   6. Identification with the Blemished . . . . . . . . . . . . . . . . . . .38

   7. Blemish and Failing Powers . . . . . . . . . . . . . . . . . . . . . . . .40

   8. The Rugged Individualist . . . . . . . . . . . . . . . . . . . . . . . . . .42

   9. The Legend of Oedipus as a Life Script . . . . . . . . . . . . . . .45

Part Two: Shame and Moral Masochism . . . . . . . . . . . . . . . . . . . .47

   10. The Therapist's Contribution to
      the Patient's Sense of Shame . . . . . . . . . . . . . . . . . . . . . . .49

   11. Depersonalization and Masochism . . . . . . . . . . . . . . . . . .62

   12. Masochist's Contempt for Those
      Who Treat Them with Respect . . . . . . . . . . . . . . . . . . . . . .67

   13. The Danger of Sadomasochism in the
      Parenting or Re-Parenting Of Psychotics . . . . . . . . . . . . . .72

   14. The Inherent Risk to the Would-Be Rescuer
      of Entrapment by Those They Would 'Rescue' . . . . . . . . . .85

Part Three: The Unconscious Communications and the
          Defensive Function of the Psychological Game  . . . . . .89
    15. The Defensive Function of the 'Game' Scenario  . . . . . . . .91
    16. The Levels of Defense in the 'Schlemiel' Game  . . . . . . . . .100
    17. Unconscious Communication, the Anal
        Reversal and the Game of NIGYSOB  . . . . . . . . . . . . . . . .103
    18. Discord Within the Confines
        of a Mental Health Agency  . . . . . . . . . . . . . . . . . . .109
    19. Gee, You're Wonderful Professor (GYWP)  . . . . . . . . . . . .114
    20. A Case Presentation Utilizing Game Theory
        and the Analysis of Levels of Defense  . . . . . . . . . . . . .119
Part Four: Psychic Structure  . . . . . . . . . . . . . . . . . . . . . . .129
    21. A Retrospective on States of the Ego    . . . . . . . . . . . . .131
    22. Fascination as a Consequence of the Confluence
        of Conscious and Unconscious States of the Ego  . . . . . . .143
    23. Freud's Contribution to the
        Concept of the Natural Child  . . . . . . . . . . . . . . . . . .150
    24. The Natural Child Re-Evaluated  . . . . . . . . . . . . . . . . .159
    25. Passion, the Natural Child and the Hot Potato  . . . . . . . .165
    26. Intuition, Cognition and Ego Structure  . . . . . . . . . . . . .172
    27. The 'Natural Child' and Schizophrenia  . . . . . . . . . . . . .177
    28. The 'Ideal' State of the Ego  . . . . . . . . . . . . . . . . . . .180
    29. Primary Identifications in the Adult Male  . . . . . . . . . . .186
    30. The Birth of the Influencing Parent  . . . . . . . . . . . . . . .193
About the Author  . . . . . . . . . . . . . . . . . . . . . . . . . . . . . .201
References  . . . . . . . . . . . . . . . . . . . . . . . . . . . . . . . . . .203

# FOREWORD

The author modernizes Transactional Analysis with ego psychology and unconscious communication theories. His perspective clarifies subtle unconscious aspects of human interactions. With careful study, more timely and precise interventions are possible. This readable survival manual should inform therapists, employers, administrators, educators, parents and anyone who interacts in dyads or groups.

James O. Raney, MD
509 Olive Way #1331
Seattle WA 98101-1743

# INTRODUCTION

"The Blemishing of the Potent Child" is composed of thirty self-contained articles and is divided into four Parts.

**Part One:**

The game of Blemish is a game defensively initiated by authorities to 'diminish' the subordinate individual. It is the widespread prevalence and commonality of this game within our society that provides the game with its cloak of invisibility. Nine articles in Part One expose the subtle and not so subtle variants of this pattern of defense as practiced by authorities.

**Part Two:**

Part Two defines the inverse relationship between shame and guilt. Five articles in Part Two will address the topic of shame and its relationship to the sadomasochistic alliance. Shame and masochistic submission are identified as the first line of defense in the neurotic condition.

**Part Three:**

Part Two provided an address to the first line of defense in the neurotic condition. Part Three provides an address to the second and third lines of defense in the neurotic condition. Pseudo-aggression comprises the second line of defense and self-defeat is the third line of defense.

Part Three also addresses the unconscious communications contained within these sets of behaviors.

**Part Four:**

Ten articles are utilized to address what would appear to be a logical evolution of Bernean ego state theory. In Part Four we follow the directive first provided by Berne when he stated that his ego state diagram and ego state theory should include a third dimension of depth, the unconscious states of the ego.

# Part One

# THE BLEMISHING OF
# THE POTENT CHILD

I began my studies in 1965. The investigation of script theory and of early life decisions based on parental programming signified to me the impressionability of the Oedipal aged child. I became aware of how crucial these years are for the formation of a sense of who and what we are. I also undertook to familiarize myself with Freudian psychology. Despite the persuasiveness of Freud's case material, as presented in his writings, my response to the Freudian theory of a universal Oedipal complex was a restrained skepticism. Further studies informed me that I was not alone in disputing the Freudian concept of an Oedipus complex.

> "Fromm points out that the recent data show that the Freudian Oedipus complex is not universal, that the rivalry between father and son does not occur in societies where strong patriarchal authority does not exist, and that the tie to the mother is not essentially sexual. When not suppressed, infantile sexuality, instead of being directed primarily toward the mother, is normally satisfied auto-erotically and by contact with other children." (Mullahy, 1955 pg. 277-78)

Even if the Oedipal complex were the innate inheritance of the individual it would seem evident that the enactment of an Oedipal complex would require a stimulus from an external source in order to become mobilized.

It is my contention that a sexual fixation on the parents does not arise from a biological drive. The fixations of the boy to the mother, and of the girl to the father arise only in response to the particular family dynamics of that particular family.

In recent years, we have been bombarded with reports of cases of implanted false memories. It is the impressionability of the child during the period in the child's life defined as the Oedipal stage of development that allow parental therapists and other authorities to implant in the patient false memories of childhood sexual abuses and seductions. This impressionable state-of-the-ego, the child within, still resides within the adult, and just as the oedipal aged child is vulnerable to exploitation and abuse, parental therapist's and other parental figures may exploit the oedipal aged child within-the-adult by implanting false memories.

Freud reported having recovered a memory of having as a child experienced sexual desires for his mother. We need to consider the possibility that there was a third party involved in the recovery of this memory. There were present the imago of the mother, Freud's oedipal-aged Child state of the ego and the psychologist Freud who was invested in demonstrating the existence of infantile sexuality.

It is the premise of Part One of this book that the conditions identified as 'castration anxiety' and as the castration complex do not arise in a vacuum. I must dispute the Freudian claim that the condition defined metaphorically as castration anxiety is the product of the child's unresolved Oedipal issues. The castration complex and castration anxiety is the child's response to a parental stimulus. The stimulus is the enactment of the game of 'Blemish.' (Berne, Eric, 1962)

The game of Blemish is a game initiated by authorities to 'diminish' the subordinate individual. It is the psychological game of Blemish, an observable interpersonal interaction, that triggers the development of neurosis and the condition defined metaphorically as "castration anxiety."

The game of Blemish is endemic in our society. It is the widespread prevalence and commonality of this game within our society that provides the game with its cloak of invisibility and allows the game to go unrecognized and unapprised.

Unresolved Oedipal issues and the condition metaphorically defined as "castration anxiety" will be defined in subsequent articles as a transactional response to a transactional stimulus.

# 1

# The Insecurities of King Laius (Lay-es)

Freud's theory of an instinctual oedipal complex defined the child's condition of feeling 'belittled' or 'psychologically castrated' as the product of the child's failure to resolve the universal oedipal issues to which all are supposedly subject. This theory was the topic of much controversy during Freud's long life.

Possibly our current theory of interpersonal interactions pertaining to the psychological 'games' that diminish or psychologically castrate others might have proven even more controversial during Freud's lifetime.

Freud chose the term Oedipus Complex to designate what he defined as the afflicted child's unresolved instinctual conflicts pertaining to their unconscious feelings of love toward the parent of the opposite sex and hatred towards their competitor, the parent of the same sex. Freud postulated that this conflict with the parent of the same sex would subsequently trigger a fear of retaliation (psychological castration) by that parent. This theory of a universal Oedipal instinctual conflict posits the assumption that the causative factors responsible for a neurosis reside entirely within the psyche of the neurotically afflicted child.

An examination of the reported history of Oedipus indicates that Freud took great liberties in basing his Oedipal theory on the story of Oedipus.

## The Ancient Story of Oedipus

Every ancient version of the legend of Oedipus and his father King Laius refers to the father's crimes against the child.

King Laius is portrayed as a truly monstrous individual guilty of many crimes including the rape of the son of his best friend.

According to Greek mythology, an Oracle warned King Laius that his own son would slay him. Accordingly, when his wife bore him a son, he physically blemished the baby by pinning his ankles together (hence the name Oedipus, "swell-foot") and abandoned his son to the elements on Mount Cithaeron with the assumption that no one would rescue the baby.

As a young man, Oedipus was traveling towards Thebes when he encountered King Laius who provoked a quarrel. Thus, Oedipus was impelled to slay King Laius not knowing that Laius was his own father. Oedipus then married the widow of King Laius not knowing that she was his own mother. Thus, Oedipus became the King of Thebes.

## A Modern Replay of the Oedipus Theme

Mr. Shane is an orderly, well-organized man, competent in his profession. He maintains a satisfactory relationship with his wife and children. Previously, his recognition that his own use of alcohol was becoming excessive prompted him to join Alcoholics Anonymous. He remains abstinent and active in the AA program.

Mr. Shane's father had taken every opportunity to blemish and embarrass his own son. A crystallizing event occurred when the boy was twelve. His father caught him masturbating and dragged him down the hall so his mother could see what the boy was doing. The father offered him, sexually aroused, to the mother. Mr. Shane experienced his mother's response as quite castrating. Clearly, both parents were experienced as castrating.

Mr. Shane's presenting problems were low self-esteem, shame and anxiety. Mr. Shane reported a larger conglomerate had recently acquired the company for which he worked. He was currently supervising his own department as well as temporarily supervising another department, the former department head having been "cut" by the new management team.

Mr. Shane reported feeling quite anxious, suspecting that the new management team was just waiting for him to make a mistake so they could 'chop off' his legs.

> "The allurement of, and fight against, passivity continues on the phallic oedipal level, too. We know from Freud that there exists a "positive" and "negative" (inverted) Oedipus. In the former, the boy wants to usurp the father's place and do all the "forbidden" things father does in the child's imagination with the mother; he "hates" the father as competitor and "loves" the mother. In the latter, the boy identifies (also under pressure of castration fear) with the mother, wants to replace her in father's affection and be sexually "mistreated" by him, as he imagines mother is: he "hates" mother as competitor, and "loves" the father." (Bergler, 1949)

The 'blemishing' of the potent child may begin in infancy and continue into adulthood. These blemishes will have a profound effect on subsequent psychic development. I submit that the passivity of the "negative' Oedipus is the continuation of passivity enforced by parental figures and that the activity of the "positive" Oedipus is a desperate attempt to rescue oneself from that passivity via enhanced aggression.

Early in treatment, Mr. Shane reported a dream of being in Europe surrounded by tall and magically magnificent buildings that he wanted to enter but was 'afraid' to do so.

The dream material and Mr. Shane's associations to the dream material 'too easily' lent themselves to an interpretation of an unresolved incestuous desire for his mother and subsequently a fear of retaliation from his father. Although the Oedipal issues in this case were quite real, the symptoms were not the result of an unresolved and incestuous desire for his mother and fear of retaliation from his father. The patient's symptomatology was the defensive response to the traumatizing blemishes that had been his lot as a child.

However, his present symptomatology was also being exacerbated by the present and very real danger that the new management team just might, at the first opportunity, "chop off his legs."

Certainly, Mr. Shane's perception of the new management team as 'castrators' could be interpreted as a manifestation of transference. However, his perception of the new management team's intentions was also quite accurate.

Mr. Shane's competence was threatening to members of the new management team, just as his competence had been experienced as threatening by his own family. Despite the blows to his self-esteem that were the product of the families Blemish games, Mr. Shane's professional and musical accomplishments had surpassed those of his father.

Treatment resulted in Mr. Shane's acceptance of the fact that those in a position of authority often feel threatened by the competence of others. He recognized that the heightened intensity of his usual symptomatology was in response to his valid perception of his supervisor's intentions.

Mr. Shane resolved his current anxiety by accepting a position with another company. This new position reduced his current level of anxiety to what he described as his 'usual' level. The new position provided him the freedom to assert his competence in productive ways and his competence was rewarded by substantial bonuses, increasing his annual income significantly. Shortly after Mr. Shane left his previous position, it became evident that the new management team had succeeded in turning their new acquisition, formerly profitable, into a money-losing proposition.

## The Laius Complex

What may be repressed from consciousness in the parent or other authority figures is their own castration anxiety, a fear of 'loss of authority' triggered by the growing potency of the child or subordinate figure. This 'authority' may be experienced by men as 'power over,' while in women it may be experienced as 'control over.' Fear of loss of this authority may prompt them to play games, to engage in behaviors that are experienced as 'castrating' by the child or the subordinate. I have come to refer to this fear of loss of authority or potency as the Laius Complex.

## The Transactional Analysis Approach to the Laius Complex: The Game of 'Blemish'

Eric Berne defined game theory in his numerous books. Berne would have defined the events that occurred between Oedipus and King Laius, and between Mr. Shane and his father, as a hard form of the game of 'Blemish.' To quote Berne:

> "The game of Blemish is played from the Depressive Child position, "I am no good," which is protectively transformed into the Parental position, "They are no good." "In its hardest form it may become a totalitarian

political game played by 'authoritarian' personalities, and then it may have serious historical repercussions. Psycho-dynamically it is usually based on sexual insecurity. Its aim is reassurance." (Berne, 1964 pg.112-113)

Blemished patients enter treatment because of anxiety, lack of self-confidence and the inability or reluctance to assert themselves in productive ways. The conclusion is inescapable that it is the parental figures who initially experienced castration anxiety, that is, the fear that their position might be usurped by the child's maturing potency. Therefore, the parental figures defend against their own castration anxiety (fear of loss of their position) by blemishing (psychologically castrating) their potent children.

In short, the child's anxiety is not a response to unresolved instinctual conflicts. His anxiety is a response to the hurtful, diminishing and, in the extreme, murderous hostility they detect in the parent.

To our knowledge Eric Berne never referred to the Laius Complex. However, his formulation of the game of Blemish clearly describes what I interpret as the Laius Complex in action.

# 2

# The Blemishing of Women and the "Sweetheart" Game

Some years ago I attended the wedding of a friend's daughter. The minister was provided by the father of the groom. As part of the marriage ceremony the minister stated, "He is obedient unto God and she is obedient unto her husband." I was appalled at this. The mother of the bride was a potent lady in her own right who competed successfully in a field usually dominated by men. She reassured me by stating, "Don't worry, my daughter will hold her own." It was instructive to note that the daughter's utilization of the game of 'Sweetheart' had a profound effect on the groom. The groom who 'was obedient unto god' over time also became 'obedient unto his bride.'

## Sweetheart

"This is seen in its fullest flower in the early stages of marital group therapy when the parties feel defensive; it can also be observed on social occasions. Mr. White makes a subtle derogatory remark about Mrs.

White, disguised as an anecdote, and ends, "Isn't that right sweetheart." (Berne, 1964 pg. 108)

In Germany during Freud's time a woman's role and position within the family and society was subservient to that of the man. Her role was to accept the subtle and not so subtle blemishes from the society of men and thereby bolster the ego of the man. The blemishing and psychological castration of women even extended to art and sculpturing of the female figure that did not include external genitalia, a vulva, a parting between the labia with the potential for an opening and for something inside.

It is my impression that women suffer from castration anxiety more frequently than from 'penis envy.'

> *"Her first tentative genital strivings suffered the same fate as all other attempts at the expression of any independence. A painful memory, from about the age of four, was of being found masturbating by the mother, who immediately threatened that if she ever did this again, mother would cut off her genitals, frame them, and hang them on the wall for all to see. The child was haunted throughout childhood by a vivid image of her labia, cut off and hung up in a picture frame."*
> (Menaker, 1953 pg. 214)

I have heard mothers rebuke their daughters with the statement, "Nice girls don't put hands in their pockets." Women's clothes designed without pockets or with pockets sewn closed have been familiar occurrences. Castration anxiety in women is often defended against by blemishing men with the assertion that it is not the women but the man who is emotionally closed and unable to be receptive or empathic and without access to inner feelings or inner resources.

> "These women are determined to believe that men are lacking something crucial; they associate the missing

something with what are explicitly described as 'Feminine' capacities."

(Mayer, 1985 pg. 33)

The blanket statement that women "suffer from penis envy" (Freud, 1938) is a blemish, an attempt to diminish the importance of a woman's genital and its capacity for receptivity. Even talented women psychologists, perhaps out of fear of losing the appearance of the capacity for receptivity, reinforced the authority and appearance of superiority of men by not publicly refuting the formulation of 'penis envy,' a formulation that they personally may give little credence.

The women that were my classmates during my initial address to oedipal issues, assumed an air of receptivity to the concept of 'penis envy,' while at the same time maintaining a mild reservation that the concept of penis envy seemed "not quite right."

I think we may safely assume that not all the women of Freud's time accepted all the blemishes including that of 'penis envy,' characterized as the lot of women, without fighting back. Wives and mothers have ample opportunity to blemish those who would oppress them, but the game of Blemish has a masculine form and connotation, it is un-empathic and lacking in receptivity. Those women who "compete," rather than "receive," are sometimes characterized as "masculine women."

The game of 'Sweetheart' has the advantage of diminishing the recipient of the game while establishing that the woman instigating the game is 'feminine' rather than 'masculine' since she is still being empathic and receptive as indicated by her referral to the recipient of the game as "sweetheart."

A man of our time, or of Freud's time, might describe to his wife how he had just completed a difficult task and how pleased he was with the results. She might respond by continuing with her tasks and with a maternal smile say in passing, "Yes dear, we all realize how wonderful you are."

Interactions such as this may have the effect of deflating the man's feeling of potency while at the same time not diminishing his perception of his wife's femininity, since she is still being 'nice.'

Blemish and Sweetheart are the same game, triggered by an unresolved Laius Complex, and instigated for the express purpose of diminishing the recipient's sense of okayness.

Although Blemish assumes a masculine form and Sweetheart assumes a feminine form, the form chosen by the instigator is probably influenced more by what they have learned from watching their parents than by considerations of their own gender identity.

## Treatment of the Blemished

The antithesis to the game of Blemish is rather simple and quite effective. First, the targeted individual must recognize that the blemisher is not operating from a position of potency and confidence, but is defending against their own insecurities.

If the targeted individual refuses to support the blemisher's position of supposed superiority and authority by becoming defensive and insecure, the blemisher is confronted with his or her own anxieties and their righteous and superior position becomes unsustainable. A simple response of, "Thank you for your opinion. I will take note of that," is usually all that is required.

One of my patients chose to take more drastic action. When she recognized the vulnerability underlying her senior coworkers blemishing, the blemisher became unsure of himself and made various errors of judgment, such as taking things out of the oven in a way that the armpit of his shirt caught on fire. Later on the same shift he caught his other armpit on fire. The following day, when he attempted to reestablish his Blemish game, my patient took out her Bic lighter and gently blew a flame in his direction. He quit his job the following day.

Patients who have a history of accepting the blemishes of others can be pretty brutal with their erstwhile oppressors once they recognize how the game works.

Once the blemished patient has accepted the interpretation of the Blemish game and how it has effected their own developing sense of self the therapist will need to move quickly to motivate the patient to learn new skills for self care. If we do not move quickly enough, the formerly downtrodden patient may be transformed into a raging and vindictive individual.

## Treatment of the Blemisher

Blemishers seldom enter treatment unless the usual circumstances of their lives have been significantly altered. Something has knocked them off balance and the underlying insecurities have become evident. Their game of Blemish may be undertaken even more compulsively, with more defensive vigor that in the past. But the game is no longer adequate to the task of sustaining their faltering self-esteem.

Probably the most dangerous intervention we can make under these circumstances is to directly confront these individuals with how they blemish others. They are dependent on the Blemish game for the maintenance of their psychic equilibrium and a premature deprivation of their game could trigger profound emotional distress. Rather than confront their use of the Blemish game for the sustenance of their faltering self-esteem and lack of self-confidence, it becomes both necessary and humane to address the lack of self-confidence now exposed. Treatment must address the lack of confidence now exposed, how their compliant acceptance of blemishing by parents and other authority figures has undermined their own self-confidence while bolstering the confidence of those who have blemished them. It is unnecessary to confront these patients with their own use of the game of Blemish. They will address this embarrassing reality in their own time.

## Conclusion

It is my conviction, based on inference rather than evidence, that Berne, who had been trained as a psychoanalyst, recognized manifestations of the Laius Complex as another example of what he defined as a "psychological game." I suspect he chose to 'not make' a connection between his theory of games and the Oedipal/Laius complexes.

Berne (1964) devoted only 39 lines to his description of the game of Blemish. His 39 lines describe the observable manifestations of the Laius Complex with brevity and a precision that is quite illuminating.

# 3

# The Invisibility of the Game of Blemish

My initial address in print to the game of Blemish was published as "The Elitism Pattern of Defense."(Woods, 1997) This article defined the organizational version of the game as it is utilized to defend the status quo of the organization or group.

Despite the widespread and frequent enactment of the game of Blemish there are experienced clinicians who are either unwilling or unable to recognize the enactment of such behaviors within their own ranks. This unwillingness to recognize the game as a game is traceable to the function of the game. The game protects and maintains the status quo whether within the family, the organization, the class or the group. Because blemishing protects the status quo, it is sometimes honored as a tool for keeping things in perspective and keeping individuals in their proper place.

A clinician from a reputable school of psychotherapy reported an example of a candidate for clinical membership being blemished. The candidate was from an impoverished background and the clinician supervising his training said, "I don't think he has what it takes." The further clinical supervision of this candidate was then turned over to a colleague. Under the supervision of the new trainer the candidate improved significantly. This improvement was rewarded with recognition as the most improved of all the candidates. However, recognition of this improvement was then blemished with the statement, "We are not sure whether this candidate has really changed or if he is just imitating what you do." Not only was the candidate's improvement being blemished but the training by his new supervisor was also being blemished.

Since the enactment of this game is so prevalent, so widespread and yet so unrecognized I must question the reason for the failure to recognize and address the prevalence of blemishing even within the field of human services. Why does the blemishing interaction, the enactment of the game of Blemish remain unrecognized as a game even by otherwise sharp-eyed observers of the human scene? What lends blemishing this cloak of invisibility?

> *It is the extroversion of the collective, the will to identify the self with the status quo (Neumann, 1954) that provides the game of Blemish with its cloak of invisibility.*

Because organizations as well as individuals utilize the game of Blemish to maintain the status quo I will review of my previously published paper on the agency version of this game. (Woods, 1997)

## The Elitism Pattern of Defense

Unresolved issues may impel individuals but also groups of individuals, movements or organizations, whether religious, psychological, political, scientific, or other to behave in nonproductive ways. One such organizational pattern of behavior is the "Elitism Game."

# The Elitism Game

A movement usually begins with the idea of one person; innovation occurs, then crystallization. The idea person is promoted to leader, then founder, and then "deity."

Individuals with unresolved insecurities may seek, idealize, and identify with a leader or a movement that provides them with a sense of personal integrity, potency, and self-assurance. Often these leaders and movements initially present themselves as accepting and open as they welcome others to join and share with them in the formation and admiration of what it is they have.

The elitists in the movement are convinced that they are the chosen purveyors of truth. This attitude is attractive to newcomers and seems to promote the movement's rapid growth. Elitists identify with their "deity" and bask in the light he or she gives off, thus alleviating feelings of personal inadequacy. Enactment of the "elitism game" does not mean that all members of a movement are equally invested in the game or that they all have unresolved insecurities. However, the unresolved insecurities of some members and their use of certain procedures to assuage those insecurities may forge a common bond that unites the elitists in such a way that they wield enough power and authority to influence policy and direction in the organization.

> *Addendum to the original article: It is the drive of extroversion, the will to identify with the collective, with the status quo, that forges this common bond.*

The game formula developed by Berne (1972, p. 23) is useful in understanding the elitism game.

**Game Formula: Con + Gimmick =Response -> Switch -> Crossup -> Payoff**
**Con:**

We are an elite. A truth has been revealed to us that make us strong, and you may share in the truth that we have.

**Gimmick:**

The desire for acceptance, to share in the truth and thus be secure from self -doubt and anxiety, and thereby to become an elite rather than a have not.

**Response:**

Membership is offered to any and all with the absolute guarantee that it will garner the new member acceptance as an elite. Membership is accepted, and the new member is instilled with new confidence and a firm belief that he or she is now an elite. Identification with the movement and the movement's founders is important, and nonconformity to the principles laid down by the founders is anxiety provoking. During this stage of the game, membership swells and the movement develops a profusion of new concepts, ideas, and services. *The Response is the period of creativity and growth.*

**Switch:**

The elitists may abuse the theory, using it as a shield to protect their self from insecurities. However, eventually old insecurities re-emerge, and faith that as an elite they possess the final word or an ultimate truth begins to erode. Discrepancies and cracks in the fabric of the movement are noticed and greeted with relief by the more secure and sober members of the movement, who recognize such fallibilities as a challenge to search for new understandings and solutions. For the elitist, however, such fallibility induces a fear that they may not be an elite after all but instead may be a have-not. To defend against this threat, elitists enact the game switch by uniting and mobilizing to take charge, freeze the movement, and protect the status quo. They discredit any internal or external factor or individual that would foster doubts or questions. The leadership now demands conformity and protection of the status quo. This may include instituting more stringent, sometimes outrageous demands on new applicants, who are more rigorously screened and frequently classified on questionable grounds as disqualified. The movement assumes a closed stance and may begin to purge itself of dissident members. The movement's totems, which symbolize reflected power and potency, are clung to even more tenaciously. *The Switch is the period of upheaval.*

*Addendum to the original formulation of this game:* It is the transpersonal introversive *will to mastery* that motivates the individual to search for new understandings and new solutions. It is transpersonal extroversion or *the will to identify with the status quo* that motivates the elitists to blemish the search for new understandings. It is the extroversive will to maintain the status quo that provides blemishing with a cloak of invisibility and precludes both the individual and the society from recognizing the blemish for what it really is.

## Crossup:

Active members who do not play the game are surprised and confused by the changes in direction, blemishing and demands for conformity. Leaders and others who play the game are surprised to discover that their demands for conformity and their effort to protect the movement and maintain the status quo is not appreciated by all the members. They are surprised to discover that some of the members have begun to question the value of continued membership in the movement. Both forward movement and creativity cease; there is a paralysis of will. *This is the period of the movement's stagnation.*

*Addendum to the original formulation:* The Crossup is that period when the will to mastery of the individual *is experienced as a threat* to a segment of the population's transpersonal will to identify their self with the existing status quo. A personalized psychology may not adequately address the need of the group to defend the status quo.

**Payoff:**
Many members withdraw from the movement. The number of new applications will decline. The movement has less appeal for energetic thinkers and self-actualizing individuals. *The Payoff is the period of the movement's decline.*

# In Summary

In this chapter I have presented an organizational version of the game Blemish. The defensive function of the enactment of Blemish must be understood in terms of personalized psychology. However, the cloak of invisibility that shrouds this frequently enacted defensive pattern of behavior becomes comprehensible when we address the transpersonal psychology of the collective. It is the extroversion of the collective that utilizes the game of Blemish to maintain the status quo. It is the collective will of the general population that provides blemishing with its cloak of invisibility.

# 4

# Blemish Within the Mental Health Field

Blemish appears to be endemic to hierarchical structures, organizations or societies. My association with the mental health field over the last thirty years has allowed me to become familiar with the game of Blemish as it occurs within the field of human services. I do not imply that the game occurs primarily or exclusively within the field of human services. I only report that it is primarily here that I have had the opportunity to observe the game and its consequences.

In a filmed interview Jung reported that on an occasion when he was analyzing one of Freud's dreams for him, he requested of Freud that he provide associations to a particular segment of the dream. Freud refused, stating that to do so would 'threaten his authority.' Fear of 'loss of his authority' could metaphorically be interpreted as, 'castration anxiety.'

In referring to this incident, Jung stated, "That was the beginning of the end of our relationship."

In this example, we may see that even Freud was subject to the effects of the Laius Complex, a fear of "loss of his authority." If even an icon in the field of psychology like Professor Freud could feel threatened by the competence of his colleagues we might well consider the effect that demonstrations of competence by subordinates might have on lesser authorities.

I once attended a professional association's conference taking place in San Francisco. An interesting and innovative approach to treatment was being presented to the packed auditorium. Standing in the back of the auditorium was a senior teaching member of the association, accompanied by several of his young followers. At the conclusion of the presentation one of his followers asked the teaching member, "What did you think of the presentation?" The teaching member dryly remarked, "Well, he certainly had a lot to say." His supercilious but unspoken attitude of "We-know-all-about-it" was not lost on his followers. His followers chuckled at the senior members unspoken implication that the presenter wasn't presenting 'new' material. Ironically, it was the senior teaching member who hadn't presented "new" material in years.

Very often the game of Blemish will be enacted in the back of rooms, in hallways or behind closed doors.

## Blemish Within the Mental Health Unit

Dr. Weider and Mr. Bono had been friends for many years. Dr. Weider was appointed to the position of Administrator of a Mental Hospital. This hospital was known to be experiencing some current difficulties. Mr. Bono took a minor staff position in the same hospital, based on his assumption that Dr. Weider would 'straighten out' the Hospital. Mr. Bono harbored the assumption that it would be informative to observe how Dr. Weider went about accomplishing this task. When Mr. Bono reported for work a coworker said to him, "It's a good thing you are friends with Dr. Weider, because I have seen the Treatment Director get rid of every potent male that has come to work here."

It became readily apparent to Mr. Bono that the treatment being provided was substandard. When the changes for the better that he had anticipated were not forthcoming, Mr. Bono made a detailed list of the Ward patients and the specific instances of the mistreatment to which they were being subjected. He then approached Dr. Weider to apprise him of the situation, fully expecting that once Dr. Weider was apprised of the situation, he would take the necessary steps to correct the situation.

Mr. Bono had made a serious error in judgment. He had failed to consider that possibly his recognition of instances of faulty treatment procedures that had escaped the notice of Dr. Weider might be experienced as threatening to the authority of Dr. Weider. Mr. Bono's second error of judgment was to accept Dr. Weider's directive that Mr. Bono make an appointment with the Treatment Director to address these concerns.

Assuming that Dr. Weider must have some plan of action in mind, Mr. Bono did make an appointment with the Treatment Director and did outline his concerns. The Treatment Director promptly fired Mr. Bono and wrote a scathing evaluation of Mr. Bono to justify the dismissal.

Dr. Weider took Mr. Bono to lunch after he had been fired and said that he could have fired the Treatment Director but then "I would have just been cutting off my nose to spite my face." Mr. Bono did not address the obvious oedipal implications of this statement.

Mr. Bono had once more made himself vulnerable to blemishing by an authority figure whose opinion and competence he had bolstered and overvalued in a repetitious reenactment of his own early oedipal drama.

Authority figures who feel vulnerable and threatened by the potency and creativity of subordinates may protect themselves by blemishing competent subordinates and then insulate themselves from anxiety by surrounding themselves with subordinates of limited ability, i.e. sycophants. Such authority figures may maintain their position of authority within an agency by taking aside each subordinate in turn and confiding to the subordinate certain blemishes pertaining to their coworkers.

Flattered by such confidences, the subordinates may each in turn offer support and reinforcement to the 'authority' of the blemisher.

I view this game with great alarm. Too often capable and talented people, sons and daughters may overvalue the authority of the blemisher and withdraw into daydreams and fantasy rather than take action and refute the blemishes. Such withdrawals, that appear to be intra-psychic and self-destructive events, are more profitably addressed as interpersonal events in which the withdrawal of the blemished individual up to and including suicide is offered as support and reinforcement for the authority of the blemisher.

# 5

# The Feelings of Inadequacy
# and Self-Inflation

In those agencies that serve our chronic mentally ill population even basically decent staff will sometimes respond to the agency clientele with blemishes in a manner that could be interpreted as 'sadistic.'

So why do basically decent and non-sadistic treatment personnel sometimes respond to their charges in this way if they are not at heart 'sadistic?'

The most frequent and most difficult to address motif for the punitive response to their charges is the defensive ego-inflation (Wiley 1989) that infests the mental health system.

In the state in which I live our leading newspapers frequently have the task of reporting the latest scandals and abuses of power occurring under the auspices of the Department of Social and Health Services.

Staff turnover in local public mental health agencies is almost epidemic. The local mental health agency in our area has a policy with the State Department of Employment requesting referrals for prospective employees who have degrees *but no experience.* Why does the agency prefer to hire those with little or no experience?

The entire mental health system extending from the State Legislature through the Department of Social and Health Services and down to the line workers who deliver basic services is currently experiencing a bad case of ego inflation. This ego inflation is their defense against the humiliating self- knowledge that they really don't know what they are doing. Highly competent individuals who manage to secure employment in such dysfunctional agencies are at risk of being 'blemished' and then 'gotten rid of.'

Frequently, those Department of Social and Health Services supervisors whose responsibility it is to insure the quality of care are individuals who have worked their way up the political ladder from the clerical pool. Too often, they have neither training nor personal experience in the delivery of care services.

During the eight years that my wife and I directed a Residential Treatment Facility (RTF) for mild to moderately disturbed young adults, three of the staff we hired realized that they were unqualified and moved successfully into other fields. Two others accepted the humiliating realization that they were not as qualified as they had assumed and subsequently worked to develop a high level of expertise, eventually moving into successful private practices. Two of those we hired, rather than face the reality of their lack of preparation, took to blemishing the agency clientele to inflate their own self-esteem. They quickly developed an "I know it all" attitude of supposed superiority and had to be let go before they did more harm.

## The Parental (Controlling) Public Agency

The object relations theorist Winnicott (1965) views developmental fixation at the symbiotic level as a result of the mother's insufficient responsiveness to the child and the manner in which aggression is handled interpersonally between mother and child.

When the mother (agency) provides a "holding environment" that contains the child's aggression without retaliation or abandonment the child can relinquish its omnipotence. When the child experiences the fact that their anger has not destroyed the mother, fantasy and reality become differentiated. (Slipp 1984) The family of the schizophrenic not only did not provide a "holding environment" to contain the child's omnipotent fantasies but even inadvertently reinforced those very fantasies.

> "Instead of presenting an opposing reality to the child's fantasies, the parents were themselves unable to handle aggression without fear of abandonment." (Slipp 1984, pg. 88)

Workers within 'the system' may themselves have an inability to tolerate the anger or aggression of the agency clientele and an inability to present an opposing reality to the client's fantasies. Such workers, to defend against an awareness of their own inadequacies may utilize the games of Blemish or Sweetheart to evacuate their feelings of inadequacy out of themselves and into their charges.

Any display of anger or frustration by agency staff or clientele may be experienced by other staff as so frightening and so dangerous that those who overtly express their anger or frustration, whether agency staff or agency clientele, are in danger of being 'gotten rid of.' The agency client's omnipotent fantasy that their angry feelings have the power to destroy is therefore reinforced. This omnipotent fantasy is accentuated in some agencies by the contagious belief that any display of anger or frustration has the potential to 'destroy' and therefore the agency feels impelled to 'eliminate' rather than 'contain' such feelings. They eliminate feelings of frustration and anger by utilizing the games of Blemish and Sweetheart to transform the feelings of anger or frustration into feelings of anxiety.

I have often observed the staff in some agencies routinely forcing the agency clientele to suppress any expression of anger or any dissatisfaction with the treatment. The expression of anger or dissatisfaction by the agency clientele may threaten the staff's inflated perception of their own competence. Staff in some agencies may routinely exorcise their own feelings of inadequacy out of themselves and into the agency clientele with humiliating references to the client's previous hospitalizations. These references (blemishes) usually start off with the statement, "You remember what happened the last time." The schizophrenic client feels humiliated by any reference to his behavior during a previous psychotic episode or any reference to his previous hospitalizations. These are painful memories for this clientele.

Mind you, these humiliating references are not delivered crudely or harshly. Instead, they are delivered with a kind and sympathetic demeanor. With practice eight hours a day, five days a week, year after year, the worker will develop a social manner that the observer might assume is the epitome of kindness and consideration even despite the unnecessary pain such interventions inflict. This type of intervention provides the worker with a sense of 'being in control,' thus masking the worker's underlying inadequacies.

The unspoken threat of being returned to the hospital effectively transforms the agency client's legitimate feelings of anger and frustration into anxiety and a sense of inadequacy. This transformation effectively maintains the patient's over-compliant, masochistic and anxious relationship to the agency staff.

## Example One

An agency staff person made a policy decision that in the future the agency would no longer wash and dry towels and bathing suits used in the swimming outings. Subsequently the agency clients would have to take the responsibility for washing and caring for their own suits and towels if they were to go on the swimming outings. The justification for this change of policy was the pronouncement that, "The clients will respond." Some of these clients were so fragmented that when not engaged they would just sit and rock, even having to be reminded to get on the bus that transported them from the agency to their living quarters. The initial result of this change of policy was a growing pile of wet and moldy bathing suits and towels at the agency. Shortly agency clients were declining the option of putting on wet and smelly bathing suits and using wet and smelly towels. This response was far different from the response envisioned by the staff person who had initiated the new policy.

Rather than admitting to an error of judgment and correcting the flawed policy the responsible staff person humiliated the agency clientele further by reminding them that they seemed incapable of washing their own suits and towels. Rather than humiliate themselves even further by admitting that they could not handle this responsibility they denied that they could not function well enough to handle this responsibility. Instead they said that they weren't going swimming anymore because they were tired of swimming. The number of swimming outings was curtailed and those who were too disorganized to care for their own suit and towel never went swimming again.

The agency clients had been placed in a double blind between making a humiliating admission or giving up the swimming activity. Their willingness to give up one of the few activities that cheered up a rather barren existence was an over-compliant and masochistic submission to the will of the staff person in question who was reluctant to admit that she had committed an error in judgment.

# Punitive Interventions

The clientele of a public mental health agency have already received so many putdowns and stays in State Institutions for assertive acts that it is very hard for them to get moving again. Anxiety and a lack of self-confidence will keep them frozen. They sit like lumps of clay, seemingly quite unmoving. Movement in these cases is quite tentative and cautions. This may be threatening to the esteem of the worker indicating that they are not as in control of the situation and the agency clientele as they would like to believe.

There is a tendency to blemish and to make the client 'bad' because of their tentative and cautious response to our efforts to 'fix' them.

# Example Two

One quite distressed agency client hitchhiked some 60 miles in an attempt to locate and see her two baby girls. Being both mentally ill and mentally retarded she had previously lost custody of her children. The loss of her children had been a painful and humiliating experience. Upon her return to the agency her caseworker bludgeoned her with the threat that if she ever attempted to see her two babies again she would be sent back to the State Hospital. The fact that this lady was really hurting did not deter her caseworker from heaping further indignities upon her.

Rather than having engaged in her customary histrionic emotional outbursts, this woman who, as I mentioned, was both mentally ill and mentally deficient, had taken self-assertive action. Her self-assertive action was narcissistically experienced as a loss of control by the caseworker. The client's success in locating the house where her two children were now living was not honored.

Often and especially in milieu therapies, self motivated changes in behavior that may be clumsy or inappropriate are never the less an indication that movement is occurring. Rather than crush this movement our response must account for such awkward and sometimes bizarre acts.

## Non-Punitive Interventions

The next two examples will illustrate interventions undertaken to support the patient's self esteem.

## Example Three

Ms. Lample was interviewed for admittance into a Residential Treatment Facility. She stormed out of the meeting shouting, "I would rather go back to the State Hospital than live in this place!" For the next two weeks this woman buzzed by the facility once a day on a motor scooter. She then dropped in unannounced, sat in the corner of the kitchen while holding one of the kitchen knives in her hand keeping it between herself and the agency personnel who continued performing the necessary kitchen tasks and duties. All of this woman's behaviors were related to as attempts at self-care and honored as such. Two days later this woman, who had a history of many psychiatric hospitalizations, moved into residence in the agency. Two years later she made a successful entry into the larger community. She has been self-supporting and free of hospitalizations over the past twenty years.

During the time this lady was in residence, with staff temporarily unavailable due to an emergency in progress, the residents had a food fight in the dining room. They then cleaned up the mess before staff returned. This incident was recognized as an unorthodox but successful means of dealing with the current anxieties including sexual tensions aroused by the absence of staff. This incident also had the effect of increasing the bonding between the residents.

# Example Four

Mr. Staple, a recent addition to the agency staff, overheard Mr. Baird make a gross sexual remark pertaining to one of the agency's female clerical staff. In a neutral and matter-of fact manner Mr. Staple informed Mr. Baird that this was not cool.

Mr. Baird then told other agency clients that he was going to 'punch out' Mr. Staple. Mr. Staple welcomed this expression of anger as an opportunity to demonstrate and reinforce the boundary between Mr. Baird's belief in the omnipotent fantasy that his feelings had the power to destroy, and the external reality that his feelings did not have the power to destroy.

Mr. Staple took Mr. Baird aside and said to him, "Look, if you're going to take a swing at me I hope you will have the courtesy to warn me ahead of time so that I have time to take off my glasses." This intervention defused Mr. Baird's belief in the omnipotence of his feelings and allowed him to back down from his threats gracefully and without losing face with his peers.

Mr. Staple welcomed incidents. He recognized incidents as the critical and most opportune time for an effective therapeutic intervention. This philosophy placed him on a collision course with the agency philosophy that called for the suppression, rather than the utilization of incidents.

Mr. Staple's supervisor informed Mr. Staple that his manner of relating to Mr. Baird was very hostile. He then took Mr. Baird aside and with a sympathetic sad smile humiliated and frightened him by informing him that if there was another incident like this he would be forced, regretfully, to recommend that Mr. Baird be returned to the State Hospital. Just as Mr. Baird's family had threatened him with retaliation and abandonment for assertive acts and genuine anger, the supervisor now threatened Mr. Baird with retaliation and abandonment. Both his family and the supervisor had reinforced his fantasy that his feelings were dangerous and must be suppressed.

Isolated incidents of blemishing and putdowns may be attributed to the unresolved sadism of individual workers. However, when an entire agency responds to its clientele with such stereotyped and gamey behavior, contagion, rather than individual dynamics, may be the culprit:

> "The sadism can be located not only in the individual but also in the theory and even in the agency culture." (Fryer, 1996)

In such a treatment environment, both staff and agency clientele may learn to relieve their frustration and anger through passive aggressive behaviors. Those workers in the field who hide their frustration, anger and hostility behind humor and laughter will be unwilling to recognize the patient's use of the same tactics.

## Example Five

Mr. Rinker was constantly interrupting his peers with his jokes and humorous asides. His peers often shouted at him to 'shut up' and to stop bugging them. Mr. Watson noticed that Mr. Rinker often held his hand over his mouth very forcefully. He asked Mr. Rinker if he held his hand over his mouth to keep from swearing at people. Mr. Rinker responded, "That's why I take my meds, so that I won't swear at people."

At the next staff meeting Mr. Watson reported his recognition of the hostile intent of Mr. Rinker's humor and interruptions and Mr. Rinker's confirmation that sometimes he had to hold his hand over his mouth to keep from swearing at people. The senior staff person responded to this report by blemishing Mr. Watson with the statement, "You really don't like Mr. Rinker do you."

# 'Blemishing' in an otherwise healthy agency

The following example is an address to the enactment of Sweetheart, a variant of the Blemish game, within the confines of an otherwise healthy agency. This example highlights the potential for disaster this pattern of behavior may have for the agency clientele.

# Example Six

Mrs. Praast was a middle-aged widow who went back to school to secure a degree. The recommendations she received from her instructor secured her a job as a counselor at an excellent agency. The agency quickly discovered that Mrs. Praast was far less competent than they had been led to believe. Supervision did not help. Mrs. Praast was unable to tolerate self-recognition of her own inadequacies. The fallout from Mrs. Praast's inability to address her own shortcomings was substantial.

Ms. Block was in remission from psychosis. She expressed an opinion to Mrs. Praast that was quite sane. Her opinion therefore deserved respect and support. Mrs. Praast sweetly blemished the opinion of Ms. Block, effectively wiped it out, and asserted her own opinion in its place. Subsequently, Ms. Block took a ride on the ferry, deluded herself that she was a mermaid, stripped to the waist and attempted to dive overboard, as she later reported, to cleanse herself. Whether Ms. Block was attempting to cleanse herself of her own opinions or the opinions of others remains an unanswered question.

The agency found it necessary to cleanse itself of the influence of Mrs. Praast before her blemishing further contaminated the agency.

# In Summary

As a defense against the recognition of their own inadequacies some workers and even some agencies in the field will utilize blemishing to evacuate the sense of their own inadequacy out of their self and into the agency clientele. The use of this procedure to evacuate a sense of personal inadequacy out of the self and into another is defined by psychoanalysis as a projective identification. Berne defined this procedure as a game of Blemish.

> "The game of Blemish is played from the Depressive Child position "I am no good" which is protectively transformed into the Parental position "They are no good." (Berne, 1964 pg. 112-113)

> "In it's hardest form it may become a totalitarian political game played by 'authoritarian' personalities, and then it may have serious historical repercussions." (Berne, 1964 pg. 112-113)

Berne also stated:
> "Psychodynamically it is usually based on sexual insecurity, and its aim is reassurance." (Berne, 1964 pg. 113)

# 6

# Identification with the Blemished

Mr. Richards, a professional computer programmer, attempted to instruct Mrs. Olin in the proper use of her home computer. Mrs. Olin seemed to have more than average difficulty in comprehending and utilizing the correct procedures. Her son was attentive and mastered the procedures by observation. He began to recognize the errors in procedure as quickly as Mr. Richards. After completing his instructions and on preparing to leave Mr. Richards heard Mrs. Olin say to her son, "Whatever you do, don't touch the delete key." Mr. Richards became very angry and in a manner that was quite uncharacteristic of him, said to her, "Don't ever say that to him again! He knows what he is doing!"

Mr. Richards reported that the boy was 12 years old, shy, awkward and intelligent and that he seldom spoke. He described the mother as a "ball breaker," a term I would define as synonymous with "blemisher."

Mr. Richards' description of the boy and his mother was also descriptive of himself and his own mother. As a child, whenever his mother had company she would behave seductively towards him, "Like we were lovers," and would then find a way to publicly humiliate him. Once, when he was six and a group of women were visiting his mother she decided to give him a bath in the kitchen sink in full view of the visitors. On that occasion and in response to her caresses, he began to get an erection. His mother snapped her finger very hard against his penis, effectively eliminating the erection. This event was experienced as, "Quite emasculating."

The mother of Mr. Richards effectively blemished and otherwise undermined her son's aspirations and efforts to be potent while offering him every enticement to do nothing with his life. The mother also blemished the father mercilessly and he had simply given up. He no longer exercised any voice in family affairs or decisions.

Mr. Richards' uncharacteristic assertiveness with Mrs. Olin was in response to his concordant identification with her son's feelings of helplessness. Mrs. Olin's attempts to blemish and otherwise diminish her own son's sense of competence and potency had enraged Mr. Richards.

Mr. Richards suffered from a condition that could be defined as a 'castration complex.' His mother's behavior toward him was at first quite seductive. Then, after arousing the boy she would humiliate him. The castrator in this family was the mother and not the father.

# 7

# Blemish and Failing Powers

Mr. Bean, an intelligent and vigorous young man, took a job on a furniture van while completing his schooling. The driver and first helper that he worked with were in their fifties and had acquired the various injuries and frailties that were the product of having spent their entire working lives lifting heavy objects. Possibly they experienced a sense of inadequacy in response to their diminishing physical capacity and the limitations in their employment options as compared to those of the younger man. Several times a day they would point out to each other that the younger man, "Doesn't know anything." By thus blemishing the younger man they were able to bolster their own faltering sense of potency. In response to repeatedly hearing this blemish day after day Mr. Bean developed an anxious and growing feeling of inadequacy. His deteriorating self-esteem induced Mr. Bean to enter treatment. Shortly after entering treatment the first helper took a position as driver of another van and Mr. Bean was promoted to the position of first helper. At group that night Mr. Bean reported his shock at hearing his self blemish the new helper by saying, "He doesn't know anything."

By playing Blemish the two older men had evacuated their own feelings of impotency and inadequacy out of themselves and into Mr. Bean. Mr. Bean had subsequently utilized the game of Blemish to evacuate the induced feelings of inadequacy out of his self and into the new helper.

The insecurities of the two older men evidenced as their own Laius complex prompted them to 'blemish' the potency of the younger man. The insecurities induced in the younger man by this game fostered in him identification with the Laius complex. Subsequently he enacted the game with the new helper.

In the pyramidal structure that is a characteristic of many organizations and groups the game may pass quickly from the very top to the very bottom of the organization. This pattern of behavior is quite contagious and may spread quickly to contaminate the entire organization.

In families the game may prove particularly virulent passing quickly from generation to generation. Those who marry into such families are also quite vulnerable to contamination by this game.

# 8

# The Rugged Individualist

During the period wherein I had involved myself with the street scene I came to be acquainted with a number of talented and competent individuals who could be classified as 'rugged individualists.' These men distanced themselves from what was going on around them. They tended to drink alone and live alone. They were alert and somewhat aloof observers of the street scene rather than actual participants in the scene. One of these men, as he observed a particular ongoing interaction, muttered a phrase in Spanish. I said to him, "I have heard you use that expression several times. What does it mean?" He replied, "A direct translation into English is not possible. The closest I can come is, "To poison with sugar." Another gentleman, observing a similar ongoing interaction said, "Shit and sugar both melt in your mouth." What these gentlemen were commenting on was their observation of an ongoing enactment of the "Sweetheart" game. Since these laypersons had each accurately perceived what was actually going on I can only assume that these two gentlemen were unusually alert to the enactment of the game of Blemish and it's variants.

Those individuals that I came to refer to as the rugged individualists were men that did not permit closeness. Therefore my understanding of the dynamics that led to their chosen lifestyle are based on extrapolation rather than any direct evidence or observation.

Mr. Duggin was a very capable man. Working from blueprints Mr. Duggin would do the layout for an entire heating system. He would then disappear for months. The company that he did this work for would put Mr. Duggin back to work any time he showed up and then got out of his way. They had learned that if anyone said anything to Mr. Duggin that could possibly be construed as a directive or criticism he would tell them to "Fuck off" and walk out the door. Because his work was so good the firm was only too glad to welcome him back whenever he chose to return.

Mr. Duggin took a day job through a temporary labor office. He was only scheduled to work that Monday but being left without supervision he accomplished so much that the owner asked him to return on Tuesday. He did such a good job on Tuesday that the owner asked him to come back on Wednesday. By Wednesday, the owner had decided that he would really like to have Mr. Duggin on his permanent payroll. Therefore, late on Wednesday afternoon, he approached Mr. Duggin with the intention of teaching him some of the finer nuances of the job and said to him, "You have done a really good job for us. However, I have been in this field for a long time and I can show you a few short-cuts that will make your job easier." Mr. Duggin responded, "Look! If you don't like the way I'm doing the job take the job and shove it!" Mr. Duggin then walked out the door. Needless to say, the owner was quite perplexed by this turn of events.

As previously stated, men like Mr. Duggin do not confide in others. Therefore, I am left to speculate as to the dynamics that would lead such a man to behave in this manner.

The individuals that I came to group under the term 'rugged individualists' were all very competent men and yet they accomplished nothing of a permanent nature in their own lives. I suspect that these men were blemished with an injunction from authority figures in their young lives that, "You will never amount to anything." They 'walk away' or otherwise sabotage every opportunity for advancement. The shame of compliantly obeying the parental injunction to "never amount to anything," Is defended against by the pseudo-aggressive act of 'telling off' every person who offers them the opportunity to fulfill their potential. Guilt for this aggression is nullified by the punishment of the lost opportunity.

I have known highly competent individuals who are 'super sensitive' to the slightest hint of criticism, are not alcoholic, and yet lead solitary lives in skid road hotels. This fact has impressed on me not only the toxic effect that "the blemishing of the potent child" may have not only on the individual, but also the tremendous loss of potential that this game induces in our society.

# 9

# The Legend of Oedipus as a Life Script

Although references to the father of Sigmund Freud are sparse, one reference I think is quite telling. Peter Gay provides us with a recounting of an incident in which Freud's father stated, "The boy will never amount to anything." (Gay, 1988)

In the previous chapter I referred to "The Rugged Individualist." It is my impression that it is the blemishing of the potent child that produces in some individuals that character trait defined as "rugged individualism."

One of the characteristics of the rugged individualist is that they tend not to listen to others who may disagree with their own ideas. Freud during his long life revised many of his own formulations. However, despite his genius, he held on tenaciously to errant and suspect formulations disputed by others. His formulations of female psychology and sexuality are a case in point.

In the past I have encountered passing references to the fact that Sigmund Freud identified himself with Oedipus. Although I paid scant attention to those references when initially encountered, upon reflection I now detect a striking parallel between the life script of Sigmund Freud and the legend of the life of King Oedipus.

An Oracle warned King Laius that if a son were born to him the son would vanquish Laius and usurp his position. When a son was born to King Laius, he blemished the child by pinning his ankles together, hence the name Oedipus (swell-foot), and abandoned the child on Mt. Citheron.

As an adult when Oedipus was traveling towards Thebes, he encountered King Laius. Laius provoked a quarrel, which forced Oedipus to vanquish his own father.

Subsequently Oedipus married his own mother and became the King of Thebes.

Freud's father provoked a quarrel by stating that Freud would never amount to anything. In response, Freud studied assiduously and became his mother's favorite. Freud thus vanquished his father becoming the family 'authority' and the King of psychoanalysis.

According to legend, a terrible plague was visited upon the kingdom of King Oedipus. This plague was the punishment of the gods to avenge the murder of King Laius. In atonement for the crime of parricide, of having vanquished his father, Oedipus put out his own eyes. By blinding himself, Oedipus alleviated the plague of guilt for his offense.

Freud, in atonement for the offense of having vanquished his own father and having assumed the father's position of authority within the family denied to himself (blinding himself) to the profound effect that the interpersonal parental interaction might evoke in the child.

Freud remained blind to the fact that his own often-reported incestuous desires for his own mother were the product of a pseudo-aggressive defense (second level of defense) against the blemishing by his father. (Bergler, 1949)

Freud remained blind to the fact that incestuous desires are not the product of a universal and innate drive (oedipal complex) but are instead the child's response to an interpersonal family dynamic.

# Part Two

# SHAME AND
# MORAL MASOCHISM

The individual by virtue of repetitious blemishing at the hands of parents and other authorities may spend their life in a running battle with passivity.

The neurotic condition consists of a three-layered level of defense. The first layer of defense, as it pertains to the neurotic condition, consists of over-compliance and masochistic submission. The child is in no position to assert their self in opposition to the authority of the parent and quickly realizes that it is prudent for them to compliantly submit. Despite, in some circumstances, the wisdom of masochistic submission as opposed to genuine self-assertion, the failure of self-actualization as it pertains to the neurotic condition may generate an intense sense of shame.

Because shame is a consequence of masochistic submission to parents, therapists and other authorities, it has received less attention than is it is due. Part Two will therefore address the topic of masochism and the sadomasochistic relationship in some detail.

# 10

# The Therapist's Contribution to the Patient's Sense of Shame

Therapists often fail to recognize that their interventions, no matter how warmly delivered, may be harmful to the patient.

I have found numerous reports in the literature detailing the patient's unwillingness, at least initially, to address their transference of sexual feelings from the positive oedipal relationship to the relationship with their therapist. These reports attribute the patient's reluctance to explore their sexual feelings for the therapist to the patient's experience of these feelings as "shameful."

*The shame prone patient is the patient who will compliantly produce whatever material will satisfy what they perceive as the needs of the therapist.* The act of submitting, of providing the associations that the therapist desires, is experienced by the patient as 'shameful.' The negation of self-interest in favor of gratifying the self- interest of the therapist will precipitate a sense of shame in the patient.

The first line of defense against the blemishing by parents or other authorities, including therapists, is masochistic over-compliance and submission. It is the masochistic submission to the parent or the therapist that is experienced as shameful.

## Psychic (or moral) Masochism

Children, in the process of socialization, submit their will to that of their parents or other caregivers. They accept parental discipline and authority as just and deserving and love their parents all the more. Given the psychic equipment of children, their needs and capacities on the one hand and their environment on the other it seems unavoidable that at least some degree of masochism will develop in the child's mind. Children who seldom receive from the parents the love, affection, and admiration necessary for the development of a sense of competence may feel vulnerable on their own. Children such as these may forgo the pleasurable experience of competence and independence for the security of masochistic submission.

The more sadistic the parent, the more likely the child is to cling to the parent and the sadomasochistic relationship. It is the fear of abandonment that drives the child to cling to others in such relationships. To maintain the masochistic bond with the sadistic other, the masochistic ego (under the aegis of the survival principle) pays the price of weakness and submission.

As a defense against the shame induced by masochistic submission, the masochist must on occasion behave in a pseudo-aggressive manner. The sadist welcomes this pseudo-rebellion as it provides them with the opportunity to re-assert their dominance over the masochist.

The masochist welcomes the punishment they receive for their pseudo-aggression as this punishment will nullify the more severe self-punishment of guilt for having engaged in 'aggressive' behavior.

"Masochism in its purest form can be observed in a dog. If a good dog, one which is highly domesticated after the pattern of the human child, is punished by spanking it becomes all the more affectionate and devoted. The good dog is to such an extent dependent on being loved by its master that it cannot resent the pain its master inflicts, nor respond in any other way but by increasing its begging for affection. Masochistic human beings often remind one of this attitude of the dog, which has become proverbial. In the beginning, all masochistic suffering was love, and the sadism of another person."

(Berliner, 1947, pg. 462-463)

"The masochistic bond is established when the ego becomes convinced that it has to pay the price of weakness and submission in order to maintain its tie with the parental imago, from which the ego expects love and restitution of its original strength. In this bond love is not possible without hostile domination."

(Bychowski, 1959, pg. 263)

Except when applied to a sexual perversion, masochism is not actually a diagnosis but rather a much-neglected factor that may be detected in normal, neurotic and psychotic individuals.

"Of the two forms of masochism, the sexual and the moral (psychic), the latter is by far the most important. It represents a definite and frequent character structure, particularly in the symptomatology of all neurotic conditions, and plays a fundamental part in Western culture. Indeed, moral masochism is so universal in human life that it was not recognized as an entity until the description of the sexual masochistic perversion sixty years ago threw a sharp spotlight on it and gave it its name. The concept of moral masochism had, historically, a bad start. The analogy with the sexual perversion obscured the fact that moral masochism is the general and basic form that furnishes the ground on which, in a minority of persons and under certain circumstances in psychosexual development, the Perversion may evolve."

(Berliner, 1947, pg. 459)

I recently observed a group of boys in animated discussion. One of the boys rushed to the street to wave at a passing car and shout, "Hi dad!" The father's only response to his son's greeting was a contemptuous (blemishing) look cast in his son's direction. Far from unhappy with this response, the boy returned to the group and proudly announced, "That was my dad." This young boy's idealization of his sadistic father was quite evident. As a stage of normal development, all children idealize their parents. This idealization of parental sadism induces masochism. Children must pay the price of submission to the will of the parents or caretakers in order to survive. This submission to the will of another at the expense of self-assertion produces powerful feelings of shame. The submission to others is experienced as less shameful when the oppressor is an idealized figure. The more children idealize their oppressors the less shameful is their dependency. In short, masochism is the idealization of one's oppressors without identification with them.

The therapist who succeeds in enticing the initially reluctant patient to compliantly supply oedipal associations indicating a sexual desire for the therapist, a sexual desire that may not exist, may have enticed the patient to repeat a lifelong pattern of 'shameful' submission to the emotional needs of others. If such is the case, the therapist has reinforced the patient's first line of defense, the idealization and masochistic submission to the authority of the sadistic other.

The patient's expectation that parents are always right and that parents may break the rules with impunity in some instances may be transferred onto the person of the therapist. This transference may trigger a counter transference response in the therapist that, "I know that in most circumstances this behavior on my part would not be justified, but in this particular situation, it is okay." The shame prone patient may compliantly submit to exploitation by the therapist without making a fuss at least initially, only later as a defense against the shame of submission, initiate a lawsuit charging the therapist with exploitation.

Feelings are highly subjective. It is difficult to convey what a feeling feels like. Therefore, attempts to identify and label shame or guilt based on the patient's reporting of subjective experience of the feeling are highly speculative and often lead to confusion.

I will now advance two working hypothesis: 1) it is the suppression of the patient's self assertive response that induces shame in the patient and, 2) that the shame prone patient's apparently guilt-free aggressive behaviors are a reaction formation, a defense against the shame of submission.

## Shame

Many previous writers make little distinction between shame and guilt and view shame as so similar to guilt both in scientific and common usage that the two terms could be considered together.

Other authorities more clearly distinguish shame from guilt. Shame is distinct from guilt and worthy of investigation in its own right.

"A psychology of the self demands that greater attention
be paid to shame; shame is to self-psychology what anxiety
is to ego psychology—the keystone effect."

(Broucek 1982 pg. 369)

Shame is related to the process of regressive merging with others and
the suppression of processes of self-assertion. Guilt, on the other hand,
is related to the processes of self-assertion and individuation.

The relationship of shame to guilt is inverse, and shame is dynamically
and developmentally distinct from guilt.

"Shame is an affect rooted in incompletely differentiated
self-other boundaries, and emerges when the primary
mode of object relations favors introjection rather than
identification as a means of internalization. In contrast,
guilt seems to require the achievement of more complete
differentiation, structuralization and internalization of
object representations. In this sense, shame is the more
primitive affect." (Spero 1983 pg. 276)

"The child learns that fitting into the symbiosis, being
what the parent wants, is rewarded by parental love,
pleasure and approval, even though this requires the
self-destruction (i.e. destruction of his own experience)."
"Activity that generates the desired parental response can
be mechanical and highly efficient, but it is essentially
unfeeling and inhuman. It is inhuman because it avoids
the critical issues of: Who am I? What do I want? What do
I think?" (Kinston 1983 pg. 217)

The child who resists the putdowns and blemishes, who insists on
being who they are rather than being who the parent wants them to be

may be rewarded with parental displeasure and disapproval that induces a neurotic sense of guilt for self-assertive behavior.

Morrison, (1984) informs us that guilt is more accessible than shame to treatment since it motivates the patient towards confession and self revelation while shame, on the other hand, reflects feelings of defect, inadequacy, and failure of the self that the patient attempts to conceal from self and therapist.

## The Shame-Prone Patient

The therapist needs to remember that the shame prone patient tends to be more attentive to the needs of others, including the therapist, than to their own needs. They may lead quiet lives of submission to the wants and needs of family and significant others in their lives. The shame the patient may experience in a submissive relationship may be experienced as a kind of misery, often diagnosed as a state of depression. It is my observation that this misery may not be relieved by anti-depressive medications. Relief does occur when the patient asserts their self and takes action on their own behalf.

## Example One

Ms. Edwards was a single mother of three. Her own mother "enjoyed poor health" and dominated her daughter to the extent that the daughter did not learn to say "no." The daughter's actions were severely constrained within the home so as not to disturb her mother. She was encouraged to spend most of her time out of the home. Her lack of self-individuation and self-assertion, in or out of the home, prevented her from saying "no" to anyone. Consequently, unscrupulous individuals had little difficulty recruiting her into a lifestyle characterized by a series of abusive and exploitive relationships, drugs and promiscuity. She experienced this lifestyle as unpleasant and "shameful."

During one treatment session, Ms. Edwards berated herself mercilessly for not submitting to the blatant manipulations of the father of her third child. Her self-abuse was in response to the neurotic guilt she experienced for saying "no." Her conflict and discomfort were relieved by the treatment group's validation that it was okay for her to assert herself and say "no."

## Example Two

Ms. Ferris, an attractive and intelligent woman of 44, had never succeeded in breaking free of her tyrannical father. An excellent businesswoman, Ms. Ferris administered her father's business and received only a subsistence salary for her efforts.

Ms. Ferris received numerous inquiries pertaining to her willingness to work for other firms. She reported, "I should leave and I feel ashamed for not leaving, but I feel so guilty whenever I do think about leaving."

Ms. Ferris had begun to engage in minor thefts from the company. These thefts alleviated the shame she experienced in response to not acting on her own behalf. These thefts were pseudo-assertive, a reaction formation that alleviated the shame of non-self assertion. Ms. Ferris was quite aware that her thefts would be discovered. She reported that once her thefts were discovered she would not feel so guilty. Pseudo-aggressive acts such as this often do not appear to induce guilt because they are essentially self-defeating. In the case of Ms. Ferris, it was inevitable that her thefts were to be discovered and that she would be severely punished. The guilt feelings one might assume Ms. Ferris would experience as a product of such undertakings, were quickly nullified by her anticipated punishment. Thoughts of asserting herself by leaving her father's company, however, generated an intense sense of guilt.

I recommend that shame prone patients such as Ms. Edwards and Ms. Ferris receive treatment in a group setting rather than in individual treatment. In a one-on-one treatment situation an impasse may develop between over-compliance and self-assertion. The patient could remain stuck in this very uncomfortable impasse for years. In a group treatment setting, identification with self-assertive peers may alleviate such an impasse, free the patient from guilt for self-assertion, and speed up the change process.

## Is it Action or a Reaction?

Every infant, every child and every adult is by nature assertive and self-actualizing unless defeated by the subtle and not so subtle blemishes that are the fate of too many. This defeat induces shame.

There are two kinds of actions that we need to be cognizant of when addressing the topic of shame.

There are self-assertive actions that are synonymous with the process of separation and individuation. Failure to engage in such self-assertive actions is experienced as "shameful."

Shame prone individuals may reactively utilize pseudo-self-assertive, aggressive, or assaultive and other self-defeating behaviors to alleviate the shame induced by their failure to take 'genuine' self assertive action on their own behalf.

> *"There are counter shame characters just as there are counter phobic characters." (Broucek 1982)*

> "It is not uncommon for a man who is ashamed of his deficient masculinity to behave in a sadistic manner towards others in order to prove his masculinity or to direct the attention of others towards his aggressive

behavior and away from his sexual behavior, upon which shame tends to concentrate. In fact, there are those who actually become criminals from a sense of shame." (Levin 1971 pg. 355)

## Example III

Unlike previous examples of patients who tended to remain stuck in shame, Mr. Davis presented the picture of a typical counter shame character.

As a child, Mr. Davis had been sexually submissive to his father and submissive in other areas as well. As an adult, he had defended against the shame of his continued lack of self-assertion by sexually assaulting his daughter. These assaults, because they were pseudo-aggressive rather than assertive acts, were doomed for discovery and punishment. Because pseudo-aggressive acts are doomed to discovery and failure, they may not induce guilt.

Several years after completing his court ordered treatment Mr. Davis entered treatment because he was again experiencing sexually assaultive impulses towards a little girl. He was also troubled by the fact that two men who had borrowed his boat had not taken proper care of the boat. However, he was reluctant to tell the two men they could no longer use his boat. I suggested to Mr. Davis that possibly his two complaints were related events. By not asserting himself with the two men who had trashed his boat, he induced in himself a sense of shame. His reluctance to tell the two men that they could not use his boat again was experienced as 'shameful.' The impulse to assault a little girl was a pseudo-aggressive impulse to evacuate the shame of submission out of himself and into a little girl.

Severely blemished individuals such as Mr. Davis typically exhibit the over-compliance and submissiveness demanded by their parental figures, transferred onto the person of the therapist. For this reason the therapist needs to be aware that although such an individual may compliantly submit to what they perceive as the therapist's directives, this compliance will be experienced by the patient as 'shameful.' Over-compliance by the patient will then impel them to reactively repeat the pseudo-aggressive behaviors that landed them in trouble in the first place.

Mr. Davis informed the two men who had trashed his boat that they could no longer use his boat. He thereafter reported that his sexual interest in little girls was in remission. In this instance, Mr. Davis had utilized self-assertion to avoid shame rather than utilize pseudo-aggression to alleviate shame. He reported feeling guilty for refusing the use of his boat, as he would have felt guilty for refusing his father. This 'neurotic' sense of guilt responded well to interpretation.

## Coping with Shame in an Institutional Setting

The Synanon program, the largest (1600 residents in California) and financially most successful of the early drug treatment programs, demanded a submissive and non- assertive stance from its residents during their everyday activities. The Synanon program institutionalized pseudo-aggression (attack therapy) as their mode of treatment. This mode of treatment was well received by the residents of the program. Verbal assaultiveness served as a defense, a reaction formation against the shame of institutionalized dependence and over-compliance.

On two occasions, in social settings, I have recognized former long-term residents of the Synanon program. Their propensity to pounce, to verbally assault, was still in evidence even after years of absence from the Synanon program.

Kaplan (1976) reports on preadolescent girls in Juvenile Court who use repellent behavior against the shame of past and subsequent confinements. The employment of scatological humor by these girls, and the efforts at projecting an "ugly" or frightening image, masks their shame.

The shame-guilt dynamic of adolescents in the judicial system creates a damned-if-you-do and damned-if-you-don't dilemma. Obedience or conformity to the norms of the family or the judicial system often means falling short of the ideal of adult independence. If they conform, they may feel ashamed of this "virtue." Self-assertion, on the other hand, often leads to a pathological sense of guilt. They may even admit to 'crimes' they have not committed to avoid the shame of conformity." (Thrane 1979)

The term 'Patsy' originated as an underworld term denoting respect. Over time the term 'Patsy' was transformed into a term of disrespect because it was the Patsy who always ended up with the stiffest sentence. The pattern of behavior observed in habitual Patsies in both the Adult and Juvenile Justice systems is habitual, predictable and repetitious.

The Patsy engages in an undertaking he or she recognize as ill advised. Initially they were reluctant to go along with the plan but allowed themselves to be seduced or persuaded to participate in a plan they recognized as not having much chance of success. Upon apprehension, Patsies, ashamed of having submitted and gone along with the plan when they knew better, and ashamed of their own lack of self-assertion, may confess to an amplified version of their own role and accept responsibility for more than their share of the undertaking. Pseudo-aggressive behaviors such as this alleviate the shame of a failure to assert the self. (Bergler 1949)

Feelings of shame, which may be quite profound and debilitating, are often misinterpreted and confused with other feelings. Most notably, they may be confused with feelings of guilt. Accurate identification and interpretation of feelings of shame requires recognition of the interpersonal context that triggered the feeling.

In any series of interactions, it may be determined whether the transaction fostered self-assertion or submission on the part of the individual. Self-assertion may or may not foster neurotic guilt in the individual but it does not foster shame.

A healthy therapeutic act may be defined as one that moves to establish a boundary between the therapist and the patient at a point where unconsciously the patient is driven into acts of fusion or merger that dissolve boundaries.

The therapist's acceptance of the patient as someone capable of addressing their own problems, of providing the patient with the necessary interpretations and then getting out of the patient's way will make it possible, if the patient so chooses, to assume an unblemished lifestyle characterized by self-assertive action and self-acceptance.

The humiliation or shame induced by a lack of self-assertion may be understood by interpretation, but the resolution of the patient's shame occurs only as a product of the patient's genuine acts of self-assertion.

# 11

# Depersonalization and Masochism

Depersonalization is defined as a loss of the sense of self. Laymen may refer to this condition as being "spacey" or "spazzed out." Depersonalization apparently functions as a defense against submission.

## Example I

Ms. Flannery, despite vigorous good health had been subjected to extensive blemishing as a "sickly" child. Concluding that her parents desired a sick child rather than a well child, Ms. Flannery would bury herself in snow up to her neck until she became quite ill. Her compliance and willingness to submit to the dominance of others continued into adulthood. Her defense against over-compliance was depersonalization. Depersonalization effectively protected her from the feeling of shame for masochistic submission and the feeling of guilt for the maintenance of good health. Profound states of depersonalization formed the basis for her many psychiatric hospitalizations.

During one of Ms. Flannery's hospitalizations, the group leader confronted her with the statement that she was not dealing with her sexual feelings for him. She replied that she did not have sexual feelings for him as she was not that grown up yet. The group leader then said, "Then why do you keep looking at my crotch?" After being informed as to what the group leader desired of Ms. Flannery, she compliantly began staring at his crotch. Several days later, another male staff took Ms. Flannery into the linen closet and raped her.

Ms. Flannery's appearance was quite remarkable and there can be little doubt that strangers would engage in sexual speculations pertaining to her person. As a defense against the shame of her masochistic compulsion to submit, Ms. Flannery would enter into a state of depersonalization. Apparently, Ms. Flannery did not enter states of depersonalization when either alone or in the company of those friends who asked nothing of her.

Ms. Flannery's profound states of depersonalization had resulted in sixty brief hospitalizations over a four-year period. When placed in an environment wherein nothing was asked of her she would quickly recover and gain release from the hospital.

Lower (1971) informs us that depersonalization not only defends against the wish to surrender in order to be loved by the sadistic other, it may also give expression to the passive wish and unconscious enjoyment of the masochistic elements in surrender.

## Example II

Mr. First was an intelligent and capable man referred for treatment because of his inability to maintain employment or function at a level commensurate with his ability or training. After some time in treatment, and during a period when his employment situation was relatively secure, it became evident that states of depersonalization, occurring for shorter or longer periods interfered with his functioning up to his full potential. During these states, he would remain vaguely aware of what was going on around him, but the conscious experience of his own thoughts or emotions as being of his own volition simply did not exist. The ego experience of a sense of his self was simply not there.

I initially speculated that his states of depersonalization might be the means by which he complied with his father's wish that he fail and not compete with the father. I soon learned that depersonalization is a regression of the ego serving as a defense against masochistic submission.

At a later date, when I observed an incident of depersonalization, I interpreted that possibly he had entered a state of depersonalization as a defense against a masochistic fantasy. He responded with the statement, "I was having a fantasy about my father shoving his cock down my throat just before I went out." As previously referred to in Chapter One and as exemplified in this example, the negative Oedipus is a continuation of the child's masochistic submission to the 'authority' of the father. In all probability, the activation of the negative Oedipus in this instance was in response to error on my part. Mr. First undoubtedly experienced my interventions as an attempt to 'shove my interpretations' down his throat. As a defense against his masochistic compulsion to submit to my intrusions, Mr. First entered a state of depersonalization.

> "The defensive significance of depersonalization may lie in the fact that it defends against the danger of surrender by a regressive retreat to an infantile negativistic state. The negative state defends against surrender by denying the wish to be loved, sexually, by the sadistic father." (Lower, 1971 pg. 596)

In order to 'cure' their self of the sense of a loss that self-depersonalization signifies, some patients may reorganize their sense of self around self-inflicted pain. The next example illustrates this sequence.

# Example III

Ms. Richter's father was a neurosurgeon who enjoyed supposedly 'hypnotizing' his daughter and sticking needles through her arms while telling her, "You don't feel any pain." He would also hypnotize her, supposedly, before having her go swimming in Puget Sound in January. Ms. Richter informed me that she could have tuned out and not felt the pain, but to do so would have been to feel that she did not exist. She was able to convince her father that she did not feel the pain even as she quietly submitted to his torture.

As a young woman, Ms. Richter learned to avoid the shame of submission by entering into profound states of depersonalization. These profound states of depersonalization resulted in many commitments.

Ms. Richter would 'cure' herself of her states of depersonalization by the process of identifying with the aggressor. By identifying with her sadistic father and mutilating her own arms with sharp instruments, she was able to reorganize her sense of self and reestablish contact very quickly. Apparently, the restitutive effects of these self- mutilations remained unrecognized during her many hospitalizations. On one occasion the hospital staff told her, "Listen, if you cut on yourself one more time, we're going to transfer you to Ward H, and that's the end of the line for you because no one ever gets off that ward!" Ms. Richter slashed her arm badly, was transferred to Ward H and from there quickly secured her discharge from the hospital.

Self-mutilation cannot be considered as an expression of masochism. It is instead a defense, an attempt at the restitution of the self from a state of depersonalization. Self- inflicted pain is a statement that says, "I hurt, I bleed, therefore *I am*." In conclusion, let us quote Edith Jacobson:

> "One more remark, concerning states of depersonalization in schizophrenics. It is my impression that in the case of chronic schizophrenic processes the experience of

depersonalization, which mostly occur in the beginning of the illness, are indicative of sudden mobilization of regressive processes. The opinion has been voiced that depersonalization represents a restitute process. However, I believe that even in psychotics it must be regarded as a defense of the ego which tries to recover and to maintain its intactness by opposing, detaching, and disowning the regressed, diseased part." (Jacobson, 1959 pg. 609)

# 12

# The Masochist's Contempt for Those Who Treat Them with Respect

In previous communications, I have stated that, "masochism is the idealization of our oppressors." A component of that idealization is that the form or manner of oppression becomes idealized as well. Not only is the blemisher idealized, but the blemishing is also idealized.

This chapter will provide an address to the futility of efforts to "cure" the masochist by offering them comfort and positive acknowledgment.

I am aware of instances wherein young and not so young men have repeatedly attempted to win the affections of masochistic women by providing them with the care and consideration that they had never previously experienced. Far from winning the affection of the masochist this particular courtship maneuver, in all the cases I am aware of, won its initiators only rejection and contempt.

# Example I

Ms. Greene was being pursued by Mr. Smythe. She had known only blemishing and sarcasm from her own father.

Mr. Smythe's courtship had begun with his search for and location of an attractive female (Ms. Greene) who had been involved in a series of abusive or otherwise dysfunctional relationships. Operating on the assumption that if he were to provide Ms. Greene with the warmth, caring and support that had been lacking in her previous relationships she would compare his treatment of her as favorable to the treatment she had received from others in the past. Ms. Greene was being pursued as well by Mr. Guardino, a man noted for his sarcastic wit and his penchant for using and then discarding women.

Mr. Smythe took Ms. Greene to a dance. He showed her only kindness and consideration. Mr. Guardino was also at the dance. As a courtship maneuver he ignored Ms. Greene. After some time had passed Ms. Greene announced that she had a few choice words to say to Mr. Guardino and then she would be through with him. She rose from the table, gently patted Mr. Smythe on the arm and reassured him that she would be right back. She then went over to the table of Mr. Guardino. Mr. Guardino apparently said something that angered Mrs. Greene. They began to argue. Shortly Ms. Greene sat down at the table and continued to argue with Mr. Guardino. Ms. Greene did not return to the table of Mr. Smythe.

Later, Ms. Greene blemished Mr. Smythe with the statement, "You're a nice guy but you're such a wimp!" She then turned her back on him and walked away. The contempt in her manner and voice was not lost on Mr. Smythe.

The expectation that others will love us if we are nice to them in many cases is quite unrealistic. The masochist may surprise the uninformed by responding with contempt to efforts to care for them. This contemptuous response may be immediate or it may be delayed for a few days, months *or even years*.

# Example II

Early in my career Mrs. Schiller, who generously provided us with much needed and invaluable expertise in both clinical and interagency dynamics, befriended my wife and me. Mrs. Schiller's diagnosis and prognosis pertaining to various situations turned out to be quite accurate and useful. We were quite impressed with her clinical expertise.

Mrs. Schiller informed us in a personal communication that she was leaving her husband of nine years because she had belatedly came to realize that "I just do not respect him." My wife and I had met Mr. Schiller on several occasions and found him to be an attractive, intelligent and caring individual.

Mrs. Schiller left her adoring husband and two adoring children and moved in with a man noted for his abrasive and abusive manner. She also presented a clinical case at a professional seminar in a manner that was quite provocative. Her professional colleagues shredded her presentation thoroughly. I was familiar with the principle players in the case, but was confused by the manner of the presentation. Why Mrs. Schiller had presented the case material in a manner that would elicit such a critical review perplexed me greatly.

The professional community that Mrs. Schiller was a member of became quite critical of her professional and personal behavior. Out of gratitude for her previous support and assistance, I continued to maintain a respectful and uncritical judgment of Mrs. Schiller. My unwillingness to respond negatively to Mrs. Schiller did not go unnoticed. Far from responding favorably to my uncritical judgment of her, upon encountering Mrs. Schiller on a public thoroughfare and greeting her with courtesy and respect she responded with a contemptuous smile and a turning away of her head.

It became clear that Mrs. Schiller would not be satisfied with anything less than a complete rejection from her formerly respectful colleagues and her adoring family. Clearly, she exhibited a belated contempt and lack of respect for those who were not critical of her.

It is unrealistic to expect to be loved by the masochist just because we may treat them with more courtesy and respect than is their usual fare. The severely masochistic individual is not capable of returning love for good deeds and may respond to such efforts with contempt.

I posit that Berne (1964) would have interpreted the efforts of others to court the masochist with kindness and consideration as a game of "Kickme." The psychoanalyst might interpret efforts of individuals to court the masochist in this fashion as a manifestation of their own unresolved masochism.

It would appear that the courtship of a masochist by another masochist is a self-defeating endeavor.

The mousy, downtrodden masochist will drop out of treatment if the therapist responds to their condition by assuming a sympathetic stance. Failure to charge the masochist an adequate fee will also prompt them to drop out of treatment. We cannot cure the masochist by loving them.

Charging the masochist an exorbitant fee, a fee that will keep them threadbare, keeps them coming back for more of the same. In addition, a confrontational approach or a tendency to ignore the masochist will hold them in treatment. They cannot get well in such a treatment setting but they will stay.

The appropriate treatment approach for this clientele begins with charging them fees that are appropriate but not exorbitant, pertaining to their income.

The most satisfying therapy group I ever conducted was a group for single Welfare mothers. All of the women referred to this group had long histories of abuse by family and others, and were currently involved in abusive and exploitive relationships. The focus of the treatment was to identify and recognize the maneuvers used by the men with whom they were involved to manipulate them into a state of submission. The masochism that prompted them to submit to the subtle and not so subtle manipulations and abuses was not confronted. Such confrontations would only have indulged their masochism.

The response to this treatment approach was surprisingly prompt. The attention given to the manipulations and games practiced by their significant others prompted them to either quickly drop out of treatment and return to their abusive relationships or it prompted them to quickly drop out of their abusive relationships and stay in treatment. Those who stayed in treatment got jobs, became self-supporting and dropped out of treatment, all in short order.

One might argue that since they had precipitously dropped out of treatment they had not been 'cured.' However, the stated goal of the treatment group was that of becoming self-supporting and off Welfare. I experienced the accomplishment of the stated goals for the group quite adequate compensation for the poor financial return that this group provided. By the time these women could afford adequate fees for treatment, they no longer experienced a need for treatment.

Masochism is ego functioning based on a principle that is beyond the Reality Principle. Masochism is ego functioning based on the Survival Principle. Our task is to encourage ego functioning based on the Reality Principle. We accomplish this task by clarifying how things work.

Efforts to initiate ego functioning based on the Pleasure Principle, to make the patient feel good, simply will not work with this clientele.

# 13

## The Danger of Sadomasochism
## in the Parenting or
## Re-Parenting Of Psychotics

With regard to a wide variety of therapeutic modalities, there have been enough reports of injuries sustained by patients and lawsuits filed against therapists to warrant the assumption that under certain circumstances therapy can be a risky business.

When working with psychotics the therapist must on occasion offer appropriate support and limit setting. The therapist who is secure in his or her own sense of competence will perform these parental functions only because it is sometimes necessary. Such a therapist is relieved and gratified when their patient exits out of dependency and exercises autonomy and self-actualization. The secure therapist does not need the exercise of power over others.

Some therapists may feel threatened by the potency of colleagues, subordinates and may even feel threatened by the patient, since the patient often knows more about their condition than does the therapist.

Such a therapist, as a defense against their own insecurities, will enjoy the exercise of power and demand submission and over-compliance from the psychotic patient. The therapist who 'enjoys' the exercise of power over patients may insist that they are doing what they do to their patients "for their own good." In reality, the exercise of power over psychotic patients is sometimes undertaken to reassure therapists of their sense of potency.

The establishment or attempt to establish a sadomasochistic relationship may occur via four scenarios.

1. The masochistic patient attempts to provoke a sadistic response in the therapist, thereby enhancing the therapist's sadism.
2. The therapist blemishes the patient in order to promote the patient's masochistic submission.
3. The therapist blemishes the patient in an attempt to provoke a masochistic response. When the patient does not readily submit the power struggle between therapist and patient may escalate to the point where physical injury results and/or lawsuits are filed.
4. The sadistic therapist and masochistic patient may form a sadomasochistic *folie a deux* that may be sustained for the lifetime of both participants.

Each of these possible scenarios is described later in the chapter, but let us begin with further considerations of psychic masochism followed by a brief review of the work of John Rosen (1953) who popularized the use of reparenting techniques for the treatment of psychosis.

## The Work of John Rosen

John Rosen (1953) began his work with individuals who were considered 'hopeless psychotics.' Berne (1969) in his introduction to Schiff's

1969 article on Reparenting, reported that Rosen's first paper on direct analysis, an article dealing with the reparenting techniques he had developed, was published in 1946. In brief, Rosen suggested that just as neurotic and character disordered individuals externalize the source of internal conflict via games, psychotics externalize the introjected image of the sadistic parent as a hallucinated voice coming from the outside. If the hallucinated voice appeared to be that of the mother Rosen would say, "I am your mother." He would then hold long conversations with the patient thus taking the place of the hallucinated voice. Via the process of introjective identification, Rosen was able to identify himself with the patient's hallucinations, take their place and reparent the psychotic with a less sadistic internalized parent. In all his writings and lectures, Rosen insisted that the therapist must function as a parent to the psychotic.

Rosen's frequent and prolonged identification with the patient's sadistic introjects may have had a cumulative effect. Over time, Rosen's treatment approach became more assaultive. Verbal abuse and corporal punishment were justified as "aversive techniques," and former patients filed lawsuits. The lawsuits charged Rosen with engaging in unethical and abusive treatment procedures. Rosen's use of reparenting techniques with neurotics also came under sharp criticism by colleagues who had formerly been supportive of his work.

Albert Honig, (1972) was a student of Rosen and continues reparenting psychotics at the Delaware Valley Mental Health Foundation. My correspondence with that organization eight years ago and more recent correspondence with Dr. Honig informs me that aversive techniques are no longer used. Evidently there are some that learn from the successes and failures of their mentors whereas others only repeat those successes and failures.

# Scenario One: The Masochistic patient's Attempts to Effect A Sadistic Response in the Therapist

The psychotic's introjected object, the internalized other, is experienced as sadistic. The punitive and sadistic quality of what has been introjected is particularly clear in those paranoid conditions characterized by coherent and well-organized delusions of persecution. The delusion that, "Someone is poisoning my food" or "The FBI is spying on me" illustrates the perceived sadism of the 'psychic presence' (Weiss 1950) of the parental imago.

As psychotic patients become better organized and their speech becomes more cohesive and less fragmented the influence and specifics of the psychic presence become more evident. Psychotics alleviate their inner turmoil by projecting the sadism of their internal objects onto an external object. The therapist or someone else close at hand may become the target of these projections. The patient then exerts pressure on the therapist or others to identify with and act-out the sadism projected onto them.

Patients may also exert pressure on other patients to respond to them sadistically. Searles describes his patients' therapeutic strivings in this regard as follows:

> "Their therapeutic techniques are outwardly so brutal that the therapeutic intent is seen only in the result. One apathetic, dilapidated hebephrenic patient of mine received considerable therapeutic benefit from a fellow patient, new to the ward, but like him, a veteran of several years in mental hospitals, who repeatedly, throughout the day, gave my patient a vigorous kick in the behind. From what I could see, this was the first time in years a fellow patient had shown any real interest in him, and my

patient as a result emerged appreciably from his state of apathy and hopelessness."

(Searles, 1975 pg. 129)

In another context, Searles described the effect that a patient's attempts to establish a projective identification may have on a therapist. In describing one of his patients he wrote:

*"Through outrageously and persistently obstreperous behavior, which involved both blatant sexual provocations as well as physical onslaughts of various kinds she eventually succeeded in fostering in me a degree of decisiveness and firmness, expressed in masterful limit setting, which I had not achieved before with anyone, either patients or others in my life." (Searles, 1975 pg. 100)*

Another of Searles patients stated, "I've had the idea for sometime that you are depressed and I've got to do something to bring you out of yourself, to get you to blow up or get you to lash out." (Searles, 1975 pg. 101)

"At one time I felt a ragefull urge to beat the craziness out of her, and I sensed this urge as similar to those which impelled her mother to repeatedly and brutally beat her daughter" Searles (pg. 123)

'Nice' schizophrenics who have given up, who live entirely within their own head, usually do not provoke abuse. However, as they attempt to reorganize themselves and externalize the sadism of their internal objects by projecting the sadism onto others, incidents or provocations that could evoke sadistic responses from treatment personnel increase noticeably. It is at this critical point that the difference between reacting to the patient versus treating the patient becomes clear. Some treatment staff may react by identifying with the sadism projected onto them, confront the patient and assume a critical and controlling stance. Other staff might choose to treat such patients rather than become confrontational. Treatment consists of recognizing, analyzing, and interpreting the defensive function of the conflicted interaction. In such cases blemishing in the form of confronting, controlling or dominating the patient is not therapeutic. Searles references to the patient's efforts to provoke the therapist are clear.

> "At an unconscious level, however, her discouragement was related also to her inability to galvanize me into being the vigorous and virile young father who had beaten her, despite year after year of contemptuously defiant, acting-out behavior and various forms of verbal incitement."
>
> (Searles, 1975 pg. 101)

## Case Example

Mr. Reise was greatly distressed by his perception that God would crucify his own son. On at least one verifiable occasion he had broken into and trashed a church. On several occasions he attempted to burn holes in the palms of his hands. Once he returned from a home visit and angrily stated, "My father acts like he's God!" This statement clearly identified the imago of his father as a sadistic God who would crucify his own son.

Once when it became necessary to restrain Mr. Reise from burning holes in the palms of his hands he became quite violent and had to be taken to the floor. He screamed "Get off me you bastard! I'm Jesus!" I decided that this was the time to expose the absurdity of his delusional system. I said to him, "If you're Jesus, perform a miracle and get me off you." His violent efforts to free himself subsided suddenly and he said, "Maybe I'm not Jesus. Are you God?" This statement illustrated his willingness to project an introjected image of his father as a sadistic God out of his own psyche and onto me. Again, to expose the absurdity of this delusion, I laughed at the assumption that I could be God. I said, "If I were God would I be down on the floor with you doing this shit?" When Mr. Reise had calmed down and had been released he thanked me and apologized for his behavior. He then stated that he was still not sure whether or not he was Jesus. I asked him, "Can Jesus walk on water? Can Jesus walk on air?" He replied that of course Jesus could do these things. I then encouraged him to get up on a chair and see if he could walk on air. Staff provided physical support and encouragement in his efforts to walk on air. The failure of his efforts to walk on air completely shattered his delusion that he was Jesus.

Mr. Reise's father was a blemisher. He played a variant of the Blemish game defined by Berne (1964) as the game of "Corner." In the game of Corner you're "damned if you do and damned if you don't." If you do the dishes you didn't do them right and if you don't do the dishes you're lazy.

> "Corner is found in a somewhat different form as a family game involving the children, where it resembles the "double bind" described by Bateson and his associates."

> "According to the Bateson school, this may be an important etiological factor in schizophrenia."

> (Berne, 1964 pg. 94)

The elder Mr. Reise had previously blemished me for his son's 'lack of progress.' Subsequently, he apparently felt threatened by his son's progress and blemished the treatment his son received with the statement, "I don't believe in all this mumbo-jumbo talk." He then pulled his son out of treatment and the son returned to his previous tours of jails and hospitals. However, the son's previous delusion that he was Jesus remains in remission.

The patient may assume a compliant and submissive role in relation to the therapist, identifying the therapist as their ego ideal as described in psychoanalytic literature. The ego ideal is the young child's idealized imago of the parent as omniscient and all-powerful. The patient derives a sense of security (although not pleasure) from establishing a symbiotic fusion with the powerful ego ideal. The therapist may feel flattered by the patient's submissive attitude and be tempted to assume a dominant role in relation to the patient. The potential for the establishment of a sadomasochistic relationship between the therapist and the patient may be an all too present danger, especially with schizophrenic and borderline patients. Symbiotic merger offers the patient an opportunity to exorcise the tortuous sadism of their internal object out of their own psyche and into the psyche of the therapist.

Therapists and other authority figures that are not sadistic may encourage separation, individuation and autonomous behavior. In contrast, therapists and other authority figures that allow their self to identify with the patient's ego ideal may play out the sadism and grandiosity projected onto them by blemishing the patient, doing themselves and the patient harm.

# Scenario Two: Sadistic Therapist's Attempts to Affect an Over Compliant, Masochistic Response in the Patient

Masochism, to a larger or lesser degree, is ubiquitous and not confined to the ranks of the mentally ill. As described earlier, it is nearly impossible to avoid the development of at least some degree of masochism in the child's early years. Later childhood and adolescence is characterized by the child's efforts to escape masochistic submission and establish autonomy. However, these efforts are not always successful, and as adults such individuals may seek the services of a therapist to complete their personal work. If the patient is fortunate enough to contact a healthy therapist, one whose treatment approach emphasizes personal growth (e.g., Goulding & Goulding, 1979/1997), then the last remnants of masochistic submission to the negative programming may be resolved very quickly.

If the patient is unfortunate enough to have contacted a therapist with unresolved sadomasochistic issues the therapist may attempt to establish themselves as the new and powerful authority in the patient's life. This authority may demand conformity and submission to the will of the therapist. The projective identifications inherent in punitive games such as "Blemish" and the variant game of "For Your Own Good" provide the means by which the therapist may evacuate their own unresolved masochism out of their own psyche and into the psyche of the patient. In this scenario the patient's own drive for separation, individuation and autonomy is depleted of authority. Patients are effectively reparented and relinquish the pleasurable experience of autonomy and independence for the illusion of security that submission to the will of a sadistic therapist may provide.

## Scenario Three: The Sadistic Therapist's Attempts to Force Unwilling or Sadistic Patients to Assume an Over-compliant and Masochistic Relationship to the Therapist

There comes a point in treatment when the patient feels threatened with losing his or her old defenses and modes of coping. The patient thus becomes defiant. Johns (1974), in his article "The Three Pots of Anger" defined defiance as anger fueled by an underlying fear of loss of self. Defiance anger may gain expression as stubbornness and arguementativeness with the therapist.

Misel referred to a similar phenomenon in terms of what he called the Gripe Stage of group treatment:

> "This stage occurs about the sixth through the twentieth session. Treatment begins to be authentically felt in this stage. Members have permission to gripe and feel. This griping is directed towards themselves, spouses, parents, and most importantly, members of the group and the therapist."(Misel, 1975 pg. 387-388)

The therapist must recognize and accept that defiance anger is a defense and also that it indicates that movement is occurring. The therapeutic task is to assist the patient in working through the fear of loss of self. Defiance anger is the patient's last effort to hold onto old ideas, and given appropriate treatment it usually proves short-lived. According to Johns (1974 pg. 19), "Patients who fit most perfectly into the defiance pot express gratitude at the identification of their anger and readily accept permission to give it up."

When the therapist fails to treat the condition and instead reactively engages in a power struggle with the patient, defiance anger may be reinforced rather than overwhelmed. If the therapist wins the power struggle, the patient's prospects for developing an autonomous and independent lifestyle may be lost forever. Such individuals may assume that the only option left is suicide. I personally know of two such cases.

The sadistic therapist may feel perfectly justified in using aversive techniques such as sleep deprivation, verbal abuse, face slapping and corporal punishment to force the unwilling patient to assume an over-compliant and masochistic relationship with the therapist. The power struggle between the patient (who may have unresolved sadistic issues of their own) and the sadistic therapist may leave the patient with physical injury and the therapist with a lawsuit. Such struggles may be terminal, ending up in the courtroom, the hospital or the morgue.

## Scenario Four: The Sadistic Therapist and the Masochistic Patient

When a sadistic therapist meets a masochistic patient the union of sadist and masochist may produce a *folie a deux* in which those who do not agree with the therapist become "the enemy." The opposition of the therapist's peers to the methods he or she uses only strengthens the therapist's hold over his or her subjects.

In Freud's 1917 account of melancholia he elaborated on the concept of the ego ideal and noted that the members of a group may take the leader as their common ego ideal and by their common attachment they identify with each other. The leader serves the function of setting standards or ideals for the group. Freud pointed out that the followers accept the leader's standard without criticism; he described the relationship in terms of the hypnotic effect the leader has on followers and the irrational nature of the "love" they have for the leader. Gear, Hill and Leido describe this process as follows:

> "In order to understand what holds each partner in the narcissistic bipolarity one has to compare the underlying anxieties that the relationship itself serves to contain. The sadistic agent fears the loss of pleasure while the masochistic patient fears he won't survive. Each variety of the *folie a deux* can be understood metaphorically as the relationship between an addict and a pusher. The agent, whether sadistic or masochistic, plays the role of

pusher, and the patient as that of his dependent addict. In the case of the borderline syndrome the addiction has simply become more obvious, approaching a symbiosis."
                    (Gear, Hill and Leido 1981, pg. 42)

This *folie a deux* may be shared for a lifetime, and over time it may become ever more paranoid in its disposition. It is masochism that prompts individuals and sometimes even groups to submissively follow and obey the will of a sadistic leader. In recent history we have seen groups of individuals compliantly submit to a leader's request that they commit murder and even mass suicide. We need only look at examples such as Jim Jones and Saddam Hussein to be reminded that the merger between the sadist and the masochist may have far reaching effects. In this scenario both patient and therapist become sicker.

## Caveat

When working with psychotics the therapist must on occasion provide appropriate support and limit setting. Therapists who are secure in their own sense of competency do not need to exercise power over the patient to bolster their own sense of potency. The secure therapist does not experience the exercise of power over others as pleasurable. They perform this function only because it is sometimes necessary. The secure therapist will be relieved and gratified when the patient exits out of dependency and exercises autonomy.

The insecure therapist may use various forms of Blemish to enforce submission and compliance in the patient. They derive no pleasure from the autonomous actions of the patient. On the contrary, they may feel threatened by the patient's display of autonomy. As a defense against this threat the therapist may escalate emotional, verbal or physical blemishing of the patient to reinforce the patient's masochistic submission. The patient's first line of defense against such blemishing is masochistic submission. This line of defense induces shame in the patient. As a defense against the shame of masochistic submission the patient, as a second line of defense, engages in pseudo-aggressive or pseudo-assertive behaviors. These pseudo-aggressive behaviors nullify the shame of the previous lack of self-assertion. However, these pseudo-aggressions induce guilt. Such behaviors are defined as pseudo-aggressive rather than as truly aggressive because these behaviors were chosen to fail. The therapist will welcome such displays of pseudo-aggression because they offer the therapist an opportunity to again exercise their power over the patient. Because the patient feels guilty for his "aggressions," the patient will gladly accept the therapist's punishment for their 'crimes' as the punishment nullifies the patient's guilty feelings.

# 14

## The Inherent Risk to the Would-Be Rescuer of Entrapment by Those They Would 'Rescue'

In a previous chapter I described four possible scenarios wherein the therapist may assume a dominant and consequently sadistic role in relation to the patient.

This chapter will address a fifth possible scenario wherein the therapist may assume a masochistic and submissive role in relation to the patient.

The initial stance of the patient bears examination. If the patient is in genuine crisis or is otherwise incapacitated it may be necessary for the therapist to take supportive action. However, there are patients who assume a dependent stance in an effort to ensnare the unwary therapist in a web of responsibility for the patient's feelings. Mr. Cordel was one such patient.

As the therapist of Mr. Cordel I found it quite difficult to remain immune to his manipulations and 'confessions.' An acquaintance of his, Ms. Groot, was not immune. Therefore, he 'confessed' to her the extent of his sexual assaultiveness and deviousness. Mr. Cordel had nothing to lose by his confession since he had correctly intuited that Ms. Groot had already been informed of his deviancy. Possibly he had much to gain. He surmised that Ms. Groot might be favorably impressed by his confession and therefore vulnerable to accepting the lies he was about to tell. He was right.

Ms. Groot was indeed impressed by his openness and 'honesty' pertaining to his deviancy. She therefore accepted his subsequent statements at face value. Mr. Cordel impressed upon her how hard he was working to recover from his deviancy, how difficult it was to change and how important her friendship was in his process of change. He trapped her in a web of responsibility for his change with the statement, "My relationship to you is very important to me as a means of changing and growing."

We are reminded of Eric Berne's description of Little Miss Muffet.

> "Little Miss Muffet sits on a tuffet feeling curdy and waiting for a Spider, which is all she can hope for. When he comes along he tries to frighten her, but she decides that he is the most beautiful Spider in the world and stays with him. He continues to frighten her periodically and she refuses to run away. She stays with him as long as she can help him spin" (Berne, 1972 pg. 220)

Ms. Groot provided Mr. Cordel with a job under her supervision. This 'supervision' consisted of masochistic submission to Mr. Cordel's entreaties to protect him from the consequences of his on the job behavior. It became necessary for Ms. Groot's supervisor to terminate the employment of Mr. Cordel. Although his on-the-job behavior had reflected badly on the judgement of Ms. Groot it must be said that she got off lighter than did some of his other 'rescuers.'

Mr. Cordel worked very hard to take control of me and the therapeutic relationship. Attempts by patients such as Mr. Cordel to force the therapist into a state of masochistic submission are very exhausting. Here are three typical statements made by Mr. Cordel. These statements were actually made as one continuous statement but for clarity they will be examined one at a time.

## Statement # One

Mr. Cordel reported that he had detected that his supervisor was someone in pain and therefore he felt 'safe' with her. He presented himself as someone who felt vulnerable. Actually, during that period, he was so defensively armored that he was quite invulnerable.

## Statement # Two

He reported that he could understand what drove a man to walk into a classroom in Canada and shoot the women. Like the man in Canada, he experienced self-assured women as dangerous. He attempted to impress on me that his assaultive behaviors were justified by his personal history and the malignant power of women.

## Statement # Three

He referred to self-assured women as "Spiders" and stated that his mother was also a Spider. His description of his own mother as a Spider was quite apt. *However, his classification of all women as being Spiders was a clear case of projection. Many were the women he had entrapped in his web.*

The efforts of Mr. Cordel to entrap me in his games made it difficult to remain objective in his case. In order to avoid becoming either assaultive or submissive I found it necessary to take vacations from the treatment of Mr. Cordel. I periodically found it necessary to say to him, "I'm tired now; I need a vacation. I won't be seeing you for another month. Come back on this date next month."

Despite how vexing and difficult Mr. Cordel could be he was invested in change and would return for treatment on the appointed day.

After years of treatment, Mr. Cordel began to identify with others and experience concern for their plight. His sadism, erected as a defense to mask his own underlying masochism, went into remission. The loss of his defensive sadism had transformed him from a hurtful individual into a very hurting individual.

The attempts of the sadistic patient to manipulate the therapist into a state of masochistic submission are exhausting. Despite the difficulty the therapist must remain neutral and objective. When this task becomes too difficult it is better that the therapist take a vacation rather than succumb to temptation. In such a situation it is essential that the therapist avoid assuming either an assaultive or submissive role in relationship to the patient. The therapist must recognize, analyze and interpret. Unless the therapist maintains their objectivity and continues to analyze and interpret the patient will have little chance of recovery.

# Part Three

## THE UNCONSCIOUS COMMUNICATIONS AND THE DEFENSIVE FUNCTION OF THE PSYCHOLOGICAL GAME

It is an axiom of communications theory that, "One cannot not communicate."

Cyberneticists, coming in one direction from theoretical physics and practical experience with communication systems and calculating machines are able to state:

> "The information carried in a precise message in the absence of a noise is infinite.

> In the presence of a noise, however, this amount of information is finite, and it approaches O [zero] very rapidly as the noise increases in intensity."

> (Weiner, 1948a pg. 78)

The psychological aspects of human communication and the mechanical aspects of communication machines are both subject to disturbance. This disturbance may be referred to as 'noise.'

> "In contrast to mathematical information, the amount of psychological information increases rather than decreases with increasingly intense (intrinsic) noise."
> (Berne, 1977 pg. 51)

What Berne referred to as "noise" is what I will refer to as "conflicted speech."

It is the conflicted speech that carries the unconscious communications.

Unconscious communications and a continuing address to the three-layered defensive structure of the neurotic condition are addressed in each of the chapters in Part Three.

# 15

## The Defensive Function of the 'Game' Scenario

The interest expressed pertaining to the Panel on 'Games' presented at the ITAA Conference in San Francisco on August 18, 1999 exceeded all expectations. People continued to pour into the overcrowded room even after a note was taped to the door saying that the room was full. The presenters each were allotted 15 minutes to briefly define their own particular philosophy or treatment procedure pertaining to game analysis. Then the presentation was opened up for general discussion.

The general discussion and panel presentation indicated that a consensus existed amongst both panel members and the audience that the term 'game' had a pejorative connotation. More importantly, there also appeared to be a consensus that the confrontation or abortion of the patient's game was not therapeutic.

It was my impression that the question that was on the audience's mind paralleled the question I had asked myself some years earlier. This question was:

> "Okay! I have read Games People Play, all the TA
> Bulletins and the early TA Journals. I am now able to
> identify and recognize the game and how it will proceed
> and conclude almost before it starts. *So now what?*"

The early history of the Transactional Analysis movement was characterized by energetic efforts to first identify and then catalog and name the patient's observable interactions with others, patterns of behavior that were defined as the patient's "game." Game recognition as outlined in the early TA literature was quite thorough and provided the clinician with ready access to game recognition. It was precisely at this juncture that game theory took what I believe was a dead-end-turn in its evolution. Game recognition evolved into game confrontation.

The combination of game recognition and game confrontation was erroneously defined as game analysis.

Subsequently, as game recognition evolved to the point where the clinician was able to identify the first move and predict the subsequent course of the game enactment, many transactional analysts took to cutting short or aborting the game rather than allowing the game to play out.

> "The ability to confront, usually with delicacy, the first
> discount easily cut short the game so formal game
> analysis seemed unnecessary."
>
> (Novey, 6/21/95)

*It is the thesis of this article that game recognition and identification, game confrontation or game aborting is not game analysis.*

# Formal Game Analysis

Significant interpersonal interactions between the patient and significant others in the patient's young life may be introjected by the patient. It must be emphasized that it is not just the imago of the self or the imago of the other that is internalized by this process but the scenario of the interaction between the self and the significant other that is internalized. The unconscious or preconscious internalized representative of this scenario between self and other provides the template upon which the subsequent interpersonal enactment of the game will be based. The game is the externalization or projection of this internal scenario onto the external world. It is this re-enactment of the individual's internal scenario transferred onto the external world as an interpersonal interaction that is identified as the patient's 'game.'

The game of "Why Don't You, Yes But" will be utilized for purposes of addressing formal game analysis.

Berne (1964) stated that the game "Why Don't You, Yes But," was the initial stimulus for the concept of games. In this game the patient asks the therapist or others for advice on how to address a particular problem. Others respond to this request with a series of, "Why don't you?" to which the patient responds, "Yes but."

# The Defensive Function of the Game

Fred's father utilized the game of Blemish to undermine any potentially assertive action that Fred might undertake. Psychodynamically, the game of Blemish is usually based on sexual insecurity, and the game is undertaken to reassure the blemisher of their own potency. (Berne, 1965) Fred would contemplate "Why don't I" undertake a particular course of action but Fred's father would vigorously blemish the wisdom of such an undertaking with a "Yes But." This frequently enacted scenario between Fred and his father had been internalized. To master the trauma of this internalized scenario, Fred projected this internal traumatic scenario onto the external environment. The role that had been Fred's in this scenario was projected onto others. In the past Fred had been the one to say, "Why Don't I?" In the present others acted out Fred's childhood role in this scenario by saying, "Why Don't You?" Fred identified with and acted out his father's role in this scenario by blemishing any possible solution to the problem with a "Yes But." In the residential setting Fred set up and played out his classic WDYYB game in its entirety. Also in residence was Susan, a woman with a history of eating disorders and hospitalizations for psychotic depression. She would sit for hours in a regressed state without speech or physical movement. In those days what I knew how to do was diagram and confront the patient's game. When the scenario of Fred's WDYYB game was confronted Susan spontaneously blurted, "That's exactly what I do in my own head all day long."

As a response to my recognition and confrontation of Fred's game he stopped playing out the scenario of WDYYB with others but like Susan, continued enacting this game scenario exclusively and compulsively on an internal plane. I then had two residents instead of just one who were compulsively enacting the WDYYB scenario entirely within the confines of their own heads.

Belatedly, I came to the realization that as a consequence of game confrontation the patient may discontinue enacting the game scenario on the interpersonal level but continue to play out the game scenario within the confines of their own mind.

As a result of the abortion of Fred's game he became less of a problem to others but he was also sicker than he had been previously.

It was at this point in my career that I abandoned game analysis as I had been trained to conduct game analysis and began searching for the unconscious meaning and defensive function of these patterns of behavior.

I now avoid confronting the game in any way that might cause the patient to prematurely 'shut down' or abort their externalization of the game scenario. The enactment of the patient's game scenario entirely within the confines of their own psyche would not only keep the patient frozen and unable to act in their own behalf but may promote a regression to a more primitive and lethal enactment of this scenario on an intrapsychic level.

The infant and young child will naturally undertake to assert themselves in various ways. If the infant's desires to assert themselves 'resonate' with the caregiver's desire for the child all will go well. It is when the desires of the caregivers for the child conflict with the infant's desires for autonomy and self-actualization that the ground for a neurotic conflict may be established.

The child is in no position to assert their self in opposition to the authority of the parent and may quickly realize that it is prudent for them to quietly submit. The neurotic condition consists of a three layered level of defense.

Masochistic submission as opposed to genuine autonomy and self-assertion is the first line of defense in the neurotic condition. The avoidance of autonomy in favor of the defense of masochistic over-compliance results in the development of an intense sense of shame.

*It is at the second defensive level of the neurotic condition that we encounter the interpersonal enactment of the psychological game.* The externalization of the internal scenario, the enactment of the game scenario on an interpersonal level defines those interactions identified by Berne as the patient's game. The pseudo-aggression of the second line of defense opposes or negates the unconscious shame induced by the abandonment of genuine self-assertion. The enactment of the game scenario as the second line of defense is defined as pseudo-aggressive because it accomplishes nothing of real value. The product of the second line of defense is guilt for the aggression.

As a defense against guilt for aggression the behaviors chosen as the second line of defense are pseudo-aggressive rather than truly aggressive. The enactment of the game scenario is therefore essentially self-defeating. The defeat that is the end product of this line of behavior provides atonement for the crime of aggression. Atonement for the crime of aggression is the third line of defense in the neurotic condition.

## Structural Considerations

Masochistic submission, the first line of defense in the neurotic condition, is a product of the parents or parental figures strong disapproval of the Natural Child's autonomous strivings. The Natural Child state of the ego is suppressed. Therefore the child over-adapts, not because they want to but because they feel they must. The Adapted Child state of the ego is born of this over-adaptation. For further elucidation, the Natural Child state of the ego is characterized by the statement "I want." The Adapted Child state of the ego is characterized by the statement, "I must."

The imago of the parental figure may be introjected by the child. This now internalized imago of the parent is experienced as the Influencing Parent. As an adult the internalized imago of the Influencing Parent of the neurotic will not distinguish between pseudo-aggression, true aggression or genuine self-assertion and is critical of all such non-compliant behaviors. The pseudo-aggression of the enactment of the game scenario earns the disapproval of the Influencing Parent. It is the disapproval of the Influencing Parent that induces guilt in the individual.

The self-defeat that comprises the third line of defense nullifies the guilt for aggression and mollifies the concerns of the Influencing Parent.

The neurotic scenario begins with the parental figure's approval of masochistic over-compliance. It culminates with the Influencing Parent's approval of the self-defeat.

# Games and Unconscious Communications

During an outpatient treatment session with Mr. Bloom, I became aware that the game scenario not only served as a defense but the enactment of this scenario also carried an encoded and unconscious communication.

Mr. Bloom's presenting complaint was that he was very lonely, that he felt rejected by his family and that when he reached out to others they rejected him. The group responded by reaching out to Mr. Bloom, offering him suggestions beginning with, "Why don't you?" Mr. Bloom rejected each of these well-intentioned suggestions. He responded to each suggestion with a "Yes but."

Mr. Bloom's presentation of himself as the one who gets rejected was in conflict with his actual behavior, behavior that consisted of his "Yes but" being used to reject others who were reaching out to him. Since Mr. Bloom's presentation of himself was in conflict with his actual behavior we may assume that Mr. Bloom was a conflicted individual.

The conflicted individual is unaware that what he says about others may be identified as an unconscious communication, identifying that which really applies to his self. What the conflicted individual says about his own self often functions as a communication mirroring his unconscious perception of the other.

People are not conflicted because they engage in interactions with others that may be classified as 'Games.' *They play these games because they are conflicted.*

Therefore, the game scenario may be recognized as an unconscious communication mirroring an internal conflict. The externalization or playing out of the patient's internal scenario with others may serve as an unconscious attempt by the patient to communicate to the therapist the exact nature of the patient's internal conflict. It also serves as a temporary respite from dangerous internal conflict.

# Interpreting the 'Gains from Games'

I formulate my task as a game analyst thusly: I analyze the defensive function of the game scenario and the unconscious communications contained within this enactment.

Does the uncovering of these levels of defense and recognition of the unconscious communications contained within the game scenario guarantee that the patient will give up enacting this scenario? *Not always!*

The patient whose lifestyle is characterized by adherence to the pleasure principle may be quite resistive to giving up the gains from illness that the enactment of the game scenario may provide.

> "Adherence to the pleasure principle motivates actions in which pleasure is striven for in an imperative and rigid way. Pain is avoided at all costs even though the avoidance or postponement of present pain will, as a consequence, result in a much more severe and painful subsequent experience of pain."
>
> (Lampl-De Groot 1965)

Some patients, whose functioning is based on adherence to the pleasure principle, become resistive to giving up the game scenario even after a thorough analysis of the defenses and unconscious communications contained within the scenario. They are reluctant to give up the instant gratification and the gains from illness that enactment of the scenario provides. The therapist's efforts to further the treatment may be stalemated.

When therapy becomes stalemated in this manner I will grin at the patient's next enactment of the scenario and in a friendly manner gently cajole the patient to describe the gains or what it is that they getting out of continuing to do this. If I have timed this intervention correctly they will grin back and describe the gains they derive from the continuance of their game scenario. Then they will put on a more serious face and attempt to replay the scenario one more time. I will quickly respond with a grin that signifies that I am aware that they are doing it again and also at the same time reassure the patient that I am not being judgmental. Their response to this intervention is usually a sheepish grin as they say, "Oh! I'm doing it again aren't I."

I undertake to address to the gains derived from the enactment of the game scenario only after completion of a thorough analysis of the unconscious defenses and communications. Also, I will undertake an address to the gains from illness only with patients whose lifestyle is characterized by adherence to the pleasure principle and only on those occasions when the treatment has become stalemated.

In my opinion, the early theory's emphasis on the gains the patient may derive from his game (gains from illness) has been largely unproductive. An analysis of the game scenario that avoids addressing the unconscious defensive function of this scenario and instead defines the gains the patient derives from the enactment of the game scenario may only reinforce the patient's self-perception of this behavior as a real aggression. Analysis and acceptance of the defensive function of the game scenario becomes far more difficult after the gains from enactment of the game scenario have been reinforced by a premature or unnecessary interpretation of those gains.

It is unnecessary to analyze the gains from illness with patients whose lifestyle is characterized by adherence to the reality principle. Instant gratification is not their goal and they may view such interventions as inappropriate and insulting.

# 16

# The Levels of Defense
# in the 'Schlemiel' Game

I have often been perplexed by the propensity of some otherwise very pleasant people to make messes. An address to the unconscious communications and the defensive function of the mess making is the topic of this chapter.

At the Christmas party at the Daycare Center, Mr. Jensen was asked to assist in serving the other guests. On four separate occasions he knocked over the drink he was in the process of serving. On each of those occasions Mr. Jensen apologized saying, "I'm sorry." Those inconvenienced by Mr. Jensen's mess making accepted his apologies and replied, "Oh! that's okay!" After the fourth incident and the fourth apology, Mr. Jensen was heard to mutter to his self, "I don't know why I keep doing this."

In the book 'Games People Play', Eric Berne reported on a pattern of behavior that he defined as the game of 'Schlemiel.' (Berne, 1964) Berne described the sequence typical of a game of Schlemiel as:

1. The guest makes a mess, spills a drink, burns a hole in the carpet, etc., etc.
2. The host grits their teeth and looks at the ceiling.
3. The guest says, "I'm sorry."
4. The host, through gritted teeth says, "Oh! that's okay!"

Although the apology has been accepted, the gritted teeth would indicate that the host is experiencing a level of resentment.

Just prior to the Christmas party in question Mr. Jensen had thrust a paper he had written into the hands of a new staff person and earnestly requested that they read the paper at the first opportunity. It was quite clear that the content of this paper held some significance pertaining to Mr. Jensen. This paper, passed to me the same day, described the resentments experienced by this country's early settlers relating to taxation and other historical events occurring between the years 1620 and 1680. The significance of this paper was Mr. Jensen's identification with the resentments of this country's early European settlers who felt that they were being unfairly taxed.

Mr. Jensen had masochistically submitted to the infantalizing efforts of parental figures in his early life. His masochistic submission had induced a sense of shame.

The mental health field has a tendency to demand masochistic submission on the part of the mentally ill. Because the mentally ill person being cared for within the mental health system must submit they are shamed by their own lack of self-assertion. Paradoxically, as a defense against the shame of lack of self-assertion, the patient may, as a reaction formation, assume the pseudo-aggressive or pseudo-assertive stance of, "I make the system take care of me." They do not long feel guilty for manipulating the system, as they pay a dear price for their dependence.

Mr. Jensen had been a captive of the mental health system from an early age. His submission to the infantalizing treatment that was his lot in life had been experienced as 'shameful.' As a defense against the shame of submitting Mr. Jensen assumed the pseudo-assertive stance of "I make them take care of me." His pseudo-assertive or aggressive stance was threatened by the efforts of others to get him to assume adult responsibilities. Therefore, these efforts were deeply resented.

Mr. Jensen was such a pleasant and likable man that others had not suspected that Mr. Jensen would resent being asked to assume an adult function or responsibility. The pseudo-aggression of his Schlemiel game had the effect of evacuating his resentment out of his self (via the process of projective identification) and into the recipients of his mess making.

Again, Mr. Mangos was a pleasant and well liked young man employed to operate construction equipment. Sometimes he would 'forget' and take home the equipment keys, thus creating messy problems for the company. He would apologize for having created a problem but continued to take home keys and schlemiel in other ways. On one occasion Mr. Magnus was told to be sure to quit what he was doing in time to get to another job site by 1:30 PM, as he would be needed at that time to operate a particular piece of equipment. Mr. Magnus was late and thus held up the entire operation for 20 minutes. This was an expensive delay for the company.

It was pointed out to Mr. Magnus that those who are resentful sometimes evacuate their resentment out of their self and into others by making a mess of things. Mr. Magnus responded, "Well! I do resent having to travel from one job to another on my lunch hour."

A variety of acting out behaviors such as the habitual lateness or mess-making behavior that Berne referred to as a game of "Schlemiel" functions as the second line of defense against the shame of non-self-assertion in the neurotic condition.

# 17

## Unconscious Communication, the Anal Reversal and the Game of NIGYSOB

In the two examples of the game of NIGYSOB (Now I've Got You, You SOB) that are the subject of this chapter I had intuitively recognized the unconscious or latent content contained within the manifest content of the patient's conscious communications. The search for an understanding of the intuitive process led to an appreciation of the unconscious communications (Langs, 1985) contained within the manifest content of the patient's conflicted speech.

The propensity of anally fixated individuals to reverse the order of the spoken word, to substitute a word that comes after for a word that comes before, was identified by Fleiss as the anal reversal. (Fleiss (1948).

This chapter will address the unconscious communications and the anal reversals that were inherent in these examples of a pattern of behavior defined by Berne (1964) as the game of NIGYSOB.

# Example I

Mr. Quint is a talented man and quite accomplished in a number of fields. He had been a precocious child who quickly and prematurely took over many family responsibilities such as paying bills and collecting rents, responsibilities that normally would fall within the domain of adult responsibility. He entered treatment following the breakup of his relationship of eight years. An articulate and attractive man, Mr. Quint had quickly found a replacement for his ex-girlfriend. Mr. Quint reported that for the first time in his life he was both impotent and not really interested in intercourse. This sudden change elicited interest but no alarm as he now preferred to just be cuddled and stroked. In response to his revelations, I experienced a vivid visual image of his girlfriend stroking his rectum. Berne (1955) referred to such images as "primal images." I do not recall ever experiencing such a vivid primal image either before or after this instance. In reference to his ex-girlfriend, Mr. Quint had said, "I still do all the homework even though she threw me out of her yard." What he had intended to say was "I still do all the yard work even though she threw me out of her home." Slips of the tongue such as the patient's reversal and substitution of a word that came after for a word that came before may be encountered and automatically corrected by the listener without conscious recognition of their significance. This 'slip' or parapraxis was recognized as an anal reversal. (Fleiss 1948)

Mr. Quint mentioned that he was doing some work for a friend of his and that he had been able to remain friends with this man for thirty years only because he insisted on Having specific instructions pertaining to what his friend required before proceeding. Mr. Quint described how his friend would give employees a free hand to perform tasks for which they were unqualified and then pounce on them for having performed the task incorrectly. Setting the employee up to perform the necessary tasks incorrectly provided the employer with a justification to pounce on the employee for doing the job incorrectly. It also provided him with the punishment of tasks uncompleted, punishment that nullified the guilt for his behavior.

The manifest content of Mr. Quint's communication was that it was his friend who engaged in this behavior. A Langsian analyst would question, "Why does the patient choose to bring up his friend's behavior at this time?" We might consider it possible that Mr. Quint had chosen this topic as an unconscious communication pertaining to his own behavior. (Langs 1985)

A characteristic of conflicted speech is that often what the conflicted individual says about others may be an encoded and unconscious communication pertaining to their self, and what they say about their self may be an encoded and unconscious communication pertaining to the other.

Inquiry verified that Mr. Quint also engaged in this pattern of behavior, a pattern of behavior identified by Berne as the game of NIGYSOB, or "Now I've Got You, You SOB." Mr. Quint engaged in this pattern of behavior with his office manager. He responded to her requests for directives on why and how to proceed on critical undertakings by telling her, "Just do it!" even though he was aware that critical factors were unknown to her. These proceedings on occasion were known to produce a crisis that threatened the solvency of his company. His initial response to crises such as this was curious. He would say to himself, "I deserve this." The offense that Mr. Quint felt that he deserved punishment for was *the verbal assault he was about to commit.*

The anal reversal, the acceptance of punishment for the crime prior to the commission of the crime is a characteristic pattern of behavior for those who have been over controlled or over stimulated during toilet training.

At this point, the previously cited slip of the tongue (parapraxis) and his propensity to accept punishment for his offenses prior to the commission of his offenses was interpreted as an anal reversal triggered by unresolved anal issues. Mr. Quint responded to the interpretation of the anal reversal by offering further material that affirmed this interpretation. He said, "That brings up something. After going to the bathroom, I would lean my head into my mother's stomach and she would wipe my bottom. She did this until I was eight or nine." Mr. Quint's current practice of seducing women to go to bed with him and cuddle and stroke him rather than engage in sexual intercourse was interpreted as his way of remembering, of acting out the tradeoff offered by his mother. (Khan1964)

Mr. Quint's mother had provided her son with excessive and inappropriate sexual gratification in exchange for his performance of duties that should have remained the responsibility of an adult.

# Example II

Mr. Levitt could be described as a sexual addict, now in remission, a drug addict, now in remission and as an active workaholic. He worked literally all the time. After finishing his workday on the job he would return home to spend evenings and weekends making improvements on his house and property. He reported that he accepted a lot of punishment from his wife if he even thought of taking some time off for himself. His wife complained that she was lonely and that he never had time for her.

I asked Mr. Levitt why was he accepting the punishment of being overworked. He replied that he did not know. I told him that it was my impression that he was accepting the punishment of overwork as atonement for something he was about to do. He responded, "I've been thinking a lot lately of telling the old lady to "fuck off" and then going off and getting loaded. I haven't done it yet because I know how it will end. I'll get loaded, then find a woman and burn myself out on her and then go on to homosexual acting out."

It was interpreted to Mr. Levitt that he accepted the punishment of burning himself out on work as the punishment prior to his commission of the crime of verbally assaulting his wife. He also accepted the punishment of burning himself out on a woman prior to the commission of the crime of homosexual acting-out. The acceptance of punishment for the crime prior to the commission of the crime was then identified as an anal reversal.

Mr. Levitt responded to the interpretation of the anal reversal by stating, "That brings up something. When I was a kid I would spread toilet paper over the toilet seat to catch my feces and I treated them as sacred objects. Lately my wife has become suspicious about how much toilet paper I use."

## The Three Levels of Defense

Mr. Quint had been subjected to over-stimulation during toilet training. Mr. Levitt had been subjected to over-coercion during toilet training. As their first line of defense each of them had masochistically submitted to an arrest in development at the anal erotic stage. The suppression of mature sexuality in favor of anal eroticism had induced in these men an intense sense of shame.

Their second line of defense was against the shame induced by submission to anal eroticism. This second line of defense consists of the pseudo-aggressive act of pouncing on others, of playing "Now I've Got You, You SOB."

This pseudo-aggressive act alleviates the shame of masochistic submission to anal eroticism, but at the cost of inducing guilt for the aggression of playing NIGYSOB.

Their third line of defense consists of having set their self up to atone ("I deserve this") for the aggression (pseudo-aggression) prior to the commission of the crime they are about to commit. In anal eroticism the fact that the third line of defense, the suffering and atonement precedes the second line of the defense of pseudo-aggression constitutes one of the paradoxes of anal eroticism.

# 18

# Discord Within the Confines of a Mental Health Agency

The daily grind and the pressure exerted on the worker in a mental health agency to respond to pathology with pathology can be intense. Unrecognized and untreated psychological games may contaminate the atmosphere and wreak havoc within the agency. Agency staff may recognize that a game is in progress yet they remain vulnerable and unable to respond appropriately.

This chapter is an address to the game of 'Chicken Little.' This game is frequently encountered within social service organizations. Organizations contaminated by the game of Chicken Little will be in a constant state of turmoil and the staff may be experiencing burnout. Failure to comprehend and adequately address the game will result in frequent staff turnover.

# The Game of 'Chicken Little'

Alan Burstein's description of the game of "Chicken Little: A game For Group Playing" (1970) is quite clear. My own experience and subsequent discussions with the staffs of other agencies confirms the conclusion that this pattern of behavior is far from rare. The supposed issues addressed in this game are often quite trivial, such as "Some patients are smoking on the porch, etc." Sometimes the issues are vague, such as "We feel uneasy and want to know why."

Burstein describes the roles in the game as:

     a. Kings/Queens
     b. Chicken Little and/or Populace

Burstein's description of the game is, in brief:

The Populace, with Chicken Little as their spokesperson, will march on the King and/or Queen to say, "Can't you see? The sky is falling!" The King and/or Queen will attempt to reassure Chicken Little and the Populace that the sky is not falling. This reassurance is rejected by Chicken Little and the Populace. Tempers rise and the exchange becomes more and more belligerent.

> "It is important to note that this game is not played from widely disparate social positions, e.g. by a ward clerk and a chief of service, but rather by people who could conceivably be allies and near peers. Chicken Little is always someone who implicitly or explicitly is sanctioned as a leader." (Burstein, 1970 pg. 9)

Out of necessity my wife and I addressed this pattern of behavior four times over a period of ten years. On two of those occasions we were cast in the role of the King and Queen. Unless this game is defused it could lead to major personnel changes within the agency.

A series of serendipitous events provided my wife and I with the information that the most important player in this drama, the actual instigator of the game, will assume a role as "Unimportant" in the game of Chicken Little. Unimportant is someone within the organization that elicits trust but has little or no authority. They present an image of being even tempered and appear to be everybody's confidant (i.e. pal).

It is Unimportant, working behind the scenes, who instigates the conflict between the King and Queen on one side and Chicken Little and Populace on the other. Unimportant will maintain anonymity as an 'unimportant' member of the gathered Populace as long as the belligerence between the combatants continues.

On our first successful diffusion of this game, we decided to "smoke out" Ms. Keys, who had been working behind the scenes to set up the confrontation. We would do this by not being hooked into the drama.

The Populace, with Ms. Ellis who had been cast in the role of Chicken Little and spokeswoman, demanded to know when we were going to do something to get them well? We quickly agreed with them that we were not doing anything to get them well and all that we provided was the opportunity. Actually getting well was something they would have to do for themselves. A lull followed our agreement that we were not doing anything to get them well. Up to this point Ms. Keys had been a silent member standing in the back of the gathered Populace. When she realized that we had no intention of fighting with the gathered Populace, she exploded with anger and strode to the front angrily demanding, "When are you going to do something to get me well?" After a brief silence Ms. Ellis, cast in the role of Chicken Little, turned to Ms. Keys and said, "You know, it seems to me that you're the only one here who is not doing anything to get yourself well." Ms. Keys rushed to her room, packed her bags and left. We were sorry to see her leave since the source of her distress, her masochistic and submissive reliance on others to get her well, had been recognized and identified by Ms. Ellis.

Eight years after this event I received a phone call from Ms. Ellis's current boyfriend. He belligerently argued that he did not think that Ms. Keys needed to return to the hospital. How I came to be a protagonist in the conflict pertaining to whether Ms. Keys should or should not return to the hospital remains unclear to me. To my knowledge I had not had contact with Ms. Keys or anyone connected with her over the intervening eight years.

The first line of defense comprising the neurotic condition of Ms. Keys was her total lack of genuine self-assertion. Her masochism and dependence on others as her caretakers was experienced by her as 'shameful.' As a defense against the shame of dependency Ms. Keys engaged in pseudo-aggressive and behind the scenes efforts to manipulate others. Guilt pertaining to the manipulation of others was quickly nullified by the fact that although her efforts were successful in stirring up a good deal of agency damage the fallout from the game always seemed to turn out badly for her as well. Two years after being contacted by Ms. Key's boyfriend I was informed of Ms. Key's death in what appeared to have been a vehicular suicide. Reports followed indicating that over the intervening ten years between my last contact with Ms. Keys and the time of her death she had apparently continued to enact this game with other agencies, creating havoc wherever she went.

It is an axiom of communications theory that you can not not-communicate. The game served as an unconscious enactment and an unconscious communication. Unconsciously, Ms. Keys had communicated each side of her internal conflict onto others who acted out and mirrored her internal conflict. Tragically, Ms. Keys had been unable to resolve this dangerous internal conflict.

The enactment of the game of "Chicken Little" is the agency version of what Berne (1964) defined as the game of "Lets You and Him Fight." The role of the instigator of the game is less obvious and more apt to go unrecognized in the agency version than in the general version of the game.

After the occasion of another successful diffusion of a game of Chicken Little Mr. Racine, who had been cast in the role of Chicken Little, asked if we would give him some feedback about the time he was involved in a barroom brawl.

Some years earlier, when he was feeling particularly lonely and at loose ends on a hot afternoon, he made his one and only visit to a topless bar. There were four or five other lonely customers watching the topless dancer. One other customer, who we will refer to as the Barroom Brawler, seemed to be having a very good time talking to the bartender and appeared not to have noticed the topless dancer. On the one hand the topless dancer probably took no pleasure at being stared at by a group of lonely, needy men. On the other hand she seemed annoyed by the Barroom Brawler's lack of attention to her. This annoyance was recognized by Mr. Racine who marched over to the Barroom Brawler and said, "You should pay attention to her." The Barroom Brawler responded by telling Mr. Racine, "Back off asshole! You don't know what's going on here!" Mr. Racine did not back off and the Barroom Brawler beat him up. During the time that the Barroom Brawler was mopping up the floor with him, Mr. Racine observed the topless dancer scrabbling around the floor on her hands and knees picking up loose change from torn pockets and overturned tables. He reported that even as he was being beat up he had occasion to think of how pathetic she looked scrabbling for crumbs on the barroom floor.

The Barroom Brawler's lack of attention to the topless dancer was a calculated maneuver that is familiar to most predatory pedophiles and to some predatory males who frequent topless bars. This maneuver consists of going to a party or bar and having a marvelous time while appearing not to have noticed the child or dancer that they want on their lap. The child or dancer who mistakenly believes that they have not been noticed will eventually climb up on the lap of the predator so as to be noticed.

# 19

# Gee, You're Wonderful Professor (GYWP)

In earlier discussions on the topic of the patient's conflicted interactions with the therapist and others, I have focused primarily on the levels of defense that may be detected in these interactions, and the unconscious communications that are contained within the conflicted interaction or game.

Projective identifications are the vehicles that convey the unconscious communication.

> "Projective identification is a psychological process that is at once a *type of defense, a mode of communication,* a primitive form of object relations, and a pathway for psychological change." *(italics mine)* (Ogden, 1982 pg. 21)

# An Unconscious Communication

Patients utilize projective identification to communicate to the therapist the nature of their distress. This communication begins with the unconscious fantasy of projecting a part of oneself into another person and of that projection taking over that person from within.

> "Then, there is pressure exerted through the interpersonal interaction such that the recipient of the projection experiences pressure to think, feel and behave in a manner congruent with the projection." (Ogden, 1982 pg. 12)

As an example of this form of communication let us consider the case of the patient who enters the therapist's office and sits or lies on the couch in such a way that her dress falls away and leaves her exposed.

Some schools of psychotherapy advocate confronting the patient's behavior. Adherents to this philosophy would tell the patient, "Pull your dress down." This confrontation will be welcomed by the patient. The confrontation, as punishment, nullifies the patient's guilt for their offense. The therapist's unwillingness to address the basic neurotic condition is gratefully recognized by the patient and serves as an invitation to the patient to play a rousing game of "Gee, You're Wonderful Professor."

Another therapist may have little interest in training or theory. He 'knows' it is the relationship between the therapist and the patient that 'heals' the patient. He may therefore ignore the patient's provocative behavior in order to avoid damaging the 'fragile' relationship. His efforts to establish 'rapport' with the patient may be experienced by the patient as an invitation to play a more seductive version of "Gee, You're Wonderful Professor."

The therapist interested in the meaning of the patient's behavior might search his or her own psyche for the unconscious meaning and communication that is contained within the patient's behavior.

"The first step of projective identification must be understood in terms of wishes to rid oneself of a part of the self (including one's internal objects), either because one feels that the part is in danger of attack by other aspects of the self."

(Ogden, 1982 pg. 12)

The therapist might note that at the moment he is trying very hard not to think about sex. Thus picking up on the projection, he may mirror the projection back to the patient by saying, "I think you are trying very hard not to think about sex."

The patient's response would be to hurriedly cover up and say, "I'm sorry, I didn't realize."

In the example just given the patient utilized projective identification not only as a defense to evacuate sexual feelings out of her self and into the therapist but also as an unconscious communication to the therapist as to the nature of her internal conflict.

The patient is naturally embarrassed by the therapist's clear recognition of the nature of her problem but she may also appreciate that the therapist has offered her an invitation to get well. Also, she will be less willing to risk her usual defensive patterns of behavior as this therapist seems to know what he is doing.

## The Game of "Gee, You're Wonderful Professor"

The experienced therapist, when reflecting on their own career may recognize a period wherein they were susceptible to a pattern of behavior known as the game of "Gee, You're Wonderful Professor" (GYWP). (Berne, 1964)

Solon Samuels related that during this period in his career:

"My patients loved my assurance and derived from it reassurance. They were grateful, and would say, "Gee, you're wonderful professor." In those days I felt very loved, and 14 carat gold stamped, as I collected my clear cut fees."

(Samuels, 1971 pg. 95)

# A Case Example

Mr. Black entered treatment because of reoccurring relationship problems, low self-confidence and a lack of self-assertion. Mr. Black was not at all resistive to my interpretations. He accepted them gratefully and after several months began telling everyone, "I have never seen my therapist make a mistake." My response to this was quite curious. I heard myself respond to this pattern of behavior by saying, "I'm excited about what you're doing." Upon sober reflection I recognized that the 'excitement' I was in touch with was not really my own. Mr. Black had first projected his unacceptable excitement out of his self and onto or into me. He had then exerted pressure on me, through the interpersonal interaction, to identify with and experience the projected excitement.

Mr. Black utilized projective identification to evacuate an unacceptable excitement out of himself and onto or into me, and secondly, to communicate to me, through my identification with his projected feelings the true nature of his difficulties, difficulties that I had failed to recognize or address up to this point.

I reviewed with Mr. Black my curious response of "I'm excited about what you're doing." I told him the 'excitement' I had experienced could not have been mine. That the excitement I had been in touch with must have been his excitement about what he was doing or planning on doing.

Mr. Black attempted to negate my interpretation by offering me diversionary tidbits but it was just too late. Each association led inevitably to the projected excitement. He recalled that as a child he was frightened of the hired man and that he was easily intimidated and fearful of men "for no reason." An address to his use of negation (for no reason) led to a report that when he was in his teens his father had said to him, "It's okay for a man to take another man once in awhile." This account was followed by the revelation that when Mr. Black was driving home from work it sometimes occurred to him that he could stop at various men's rooms along the way to engage in homosexual activities.

The unconscious content of Mr. Black's statement that, "I have never seen my therapist make a mistake," was in reality an unconscious communication signifying that up to this point the therapist had never seen Mr. Black make a mistake. Up to this point Mr. Black had been successfully concealing his 'excitement' pertaining to homosexual activity.

The 'unacceptable' excitement pertaining to these activities first projected onto me and subsequently 'identified with' by me, served not only as an unconscious defense, but also served as an unconscious communication.

"Gee, You're Wonderful Professor" is a pseudo-aggressive game. As long as the patient is successfully manipulating the therapist with this game the patient cannot get well. The patient pays the price of not getting well as punishment for their pseudo-aggressive manipulation of the therapist.

In conclusion, let me reiterate my own personal experience that when the patient has responded to me by intimating, "Gee, You're Wonderful Professor," this response appears to have been triggered by my failure to recognize and address the unconscious communications contained within the patient's use of projective identification. In retrospect I have come to recognize that it was on those occasions when I had failed to recognize and address the patient's use of projective identification and the unconscious communications they conveyed, that the patient was most apt to say to me, "Gee, You're Wonderful Professor."

# 20

# A Case Presentation Utilizing Game Theory and the Analysis of Levels of Defense

The first level of defense against blemishing by parents or other authority figures consists of masochistic over-compliance and submission to the blemishing. The byproduct of this submission is a sense of shame.

The second level of defense is against the shame of masochistic submission. This defense consists of pseudo-aggressive behaviors such as assuming a defiant or aggressive attitude in those situations wherein tact would be more appropriate. These uncalled for aggressions, more appropriately defined as pseudo-aggressions, induce guilt.

The third level of defense is against guilt for aggression. As a defense against guilt for aggression the behaviors are pseudo- aggressive rather than truly aggressive. These behaviors are chosen because they are essentially self-defeating and will subject the neurotic to punishment, punishment that will alleviate their sense of guilt.

Mr. Adams case presented a picture of both character disorder and a neurotic condition. The levels of defense that characterized the neurotic condition in this case are the primary focus of this chapter.

Mr. Adams was an articulate, attractive, and intelligent man in his early thirties. The therapist first approached by Mr. Adams saw him only once. Mr. Adams reported that he sought treatment because he had been at a dance studio with high ceilings and that the room partitions were only about seven feet high. He reported that there was a stepladder beside the wall of the dressing room and that he could easily have used the stepladder to peek at the female dancer when she went back to change. He then stated that he was fearful that he might become another Ted Bundy. The therapist referred Mr. Adams to another therapist.

When interviewed by the second therapist, Mr. Adams curled up on the floor at her feet and gave her his most 'bewitching' smile. The second therapist found the "weirdness" of Mr. Adams frightening and disruptive. She referred him to me.

To me, Mr. Adams presented a plausible picture of himself as 'dangerous.' Actually, Mr. Adams was quite provocative and presented a far greater danger to himself than to others.

During his first interview with me he presented himself as feeling powerless and fearful that he might become another Ted Bundy. He then stated, "I'm going to become the greatest television personality ever. When the money starts rolling in I'm going to open food stores all over the country where poor people will be able to get food free and I'm going to develop residential treatment facilities for all the mentally ill." He also reassured me that a position would be provided for me within his mental health organization.

The switch from feeling powerless and fearful to illusions of grandiosity was sudden and startling. Shortly thereafter Mr. Adams confessed to compulsive flashing and obscene phone calling. I was not surprised by the fact that he confessed to these crimes. It has been my experience that the exhibitionist and the obscene phone caller cannot long resist 'flashing' this confession in the face of the therapist. What I did not realize until much, much later, was that Mr. Adams did not begin his career of flashing and obscene phone calling until *after* he had begun treatment with me. He reported that when he was three or four years of age he had ran his hand up under the skirt of his baby sitter and caressed her pubic area. The baby sitter nicknamed him 'Trouble.' The nickname stuck as he continued to be trouble to family, friends, the general public and numerous governmental agencies. During his latency, Mr. Adams ran his hand up the shorts of an adult male in the park.

In the grandiose state Mr. Adams had a seeming inexhaustible appetite for the sexual conquest of women. When the grandiosity failed him he was sexually submissive to men. During the early days of our work together an older homosexual male was successfully exploiting Mr. Adams for sex, labor and money.

In one of our early therapy sessions, Mr. Adams succeeded in 'hooking' me into blemishing him.

In the first of the two sessions now under consideration, Mr. Adams exhibited a passive-aggressive (pseudo-aggressive) and hostile attitude. My response to his provocations was critical and judgmental.

I recognized the fact that I had lost my way and was responding to pathology (the patient's second line of defense) with pathology. Having lost the capacity for objective self-analysis of my own contribution to this debacle, following the initial session, I utilized the Bernean Game Formula (Berne 1972) in order to record my subjective and objective experience of the pathological interaction.

A mechanical formula such as the Bernean Game Formula is useful and sometime a necessity if the therapist is to exit out of his own pathological response to the patient.

Analysis utilizing the game formula to address my own pathological response to the provocations of Mr. Adams allowed me to switch from the critical and judgmental position that characterized the previous session to a neutral and objective position in the following session.

**Con + Gimmick = Response -> Switch -> Cross up -> Payoff**

The Bernean Game formula (Berne 1972 pgs. 23-25) states that the **Con** plus a **Gimmick** equals a **Response**. The Con in this formulation is an unconscious dynamic in one participant that acts as a Hook to another participant in the game. The Gimmick is the unconscious dynamic within the respondent that would cause them to 'Swallow' the Hook. The Response is the observable behaviors that are the product of the intermingling of the combination of Con plus Gimmick.

**Con**—Mr. Adams unconscious propensity to provoke abuse.
**Gimmick**—The therapist's unconscious propensity to respond critically.

**Response:**

> **Patient:** "I don't know why I'm here. I still get in a lot of trouble. I'm running all kinds of games on ladies. I feel like flashing a lot. I come really close sometimes. It really bothers me that my mother programmed me to be trouble. I can't seem to give up being trouble."
> *Mr. Adams had not only informed me that he expected to be abused but had provided information to entice the abuse.*
>
> **Therapist:** *"Are you ever going to stand up to your mother and give up being trouble?"*
>
> **Patient:** "I want to give it up and I'm trying to give it up."
>
> **Therapist:** "So now you're being trouble to me. You're not responding to the question I asked."
> *The more critical I became with Mr. Adams, the more uncomfortable I became with my own abusiveness, while at the same time Mr. Adams was becoming ever more*

*comfortable with my abuse of him. The abuse of Mr. Adams nullified his guilt for aggressions and provided him with his third line of defense.*

To conclude the Bernean game formula, the **Response** is followed by the game **Switch,** which is followed by the **Crossup** and concluded with the game **Payoff.** The Switch occurs when the patient and therapist switch roles. In this instance the patient (Mr. Adams) switched from the role of Victim to the role of Persecutor. The therapist switched from the role of Persecutor to the role of Victim. The Crossup is that moment of mental confusion and feeling of surprise following the Switch. The **Payoff** is the conclusion of the game and the respective gains derived by each party to "The Game."

**Switch:**

> **Patient:** "Yeah! I'm never straight with anyone. I con ladies all the time. Last night I gave this lady a complete body massage." (an account of almost assault)
> *Mr. Adams was no longer feeling helpless. It was now the therapist who was feeling helpless to exit out of the abusive role he had assumed with the patient.*
> "What I never told you before. I really respect my mother. She is a strong woman. She raised four children by herself."
> *The patient was really referring to the therapist rather than to his mother. As the therapist I had succumbed to the patient's provocations, acting-out the role of the sadistic other in his life. The pathological behavior of the therapist was gratefully received by the patient as it nullified the patient's feelings of guilt.*

**Cross up**

> At this point I had become a confused therapist and stated, "She is a strong woman and she controls you. You are still symbiotic with your mother."
>
> *It may be inferred from the previous transaction that on an unconscious level I was aware of being controlled by the patient. On a conscious level I recognized that I had gotten into something I did not understand, something I felt helpless to exit out of.*
>
> *The patient was aware that, at the present moment, I felt helpless but was not helpless.*

**Payoff**

> **Patient:** "Yeah! When I went through Lifespring they hung a nametag on me that said 'Nowhere Man' on it. That's me! I'm 'Nowhere man."
>
> **Therapist:** "When you flash, you're being nowhere."

Upon reviewing this material utilizing the Game Formula I tentatively surmised that perhaps it was the therapist, not Mr. Adams, who was 'nowhere.' Verification for this interpretation was provided at the next group session. It was one of the hottest days of the year and everyone, myself included, was wearing a T-shirt. All of the T-shirts except mine had designs or slogans printed on them. Mr. Adams said, "Look! Our therapist has nothing written on his T-shirt. He's nowhere!" He then provided further associations that further verified this interpretation.

Mr. Adams said, "When I was sexually abused as a kid I would tell myself that these guys are really nowhere or they wouldn't be doing this to me. Now when I get people to kick me I tell myself that they are really nowhere or they wouldn't be doing this to me." Although the acting out and self-defeating behaviors of Mr. Adams were the initial focus of attention, he also was quite confused pertaining to the issue of his own sexual identity. When Mr. Adams looked in the mirror he expected to see a beautiful woman. He had accessed plastic surgery to more closely approximate this expectation. He described a family portrait that symbolized his perception of the fusion of the male and female genitalia. "In the photo, I was standing in front of my mother between her legs and I had a Teddy bear on each side of me."

I had to ask myself, "Of all the things Mr. Adams could have told me why was it so important to tell me this?" I inferred that this was an unconscious communication that he had been placed between his mother's legs. One might also consider the possibility that, to the mother, he is the mother's penis.

For some time Mr. Adams maintained the delusion that women actually have a penis inside of them and believed that on one occasion he actually saw the penis when he looked inside.

Mr. Adams was quite clever and very articulate. Despite the level of his disturbance he was able to present, for brief periods of time, an illusion of competence that would enable him to acquire short terms of employment.

During a period while he was maintaining a brief employment Mr. Adams described how he always smiled at the pretty ladies at work and would get them to smile back at him. This was interpreted as a mirror-transference; when they smiled back at him he saw a reflection of himself as a pretty lady.

After some reminiscences pertaining to his childhood Mr. Adams reported that on his way to my office a pretty lady had sat across the aisle from him and when she looked at him her eyes were dull and dead. She left the bus just as another pretty lady was getting on the bus and they had smiled at each other. He reported feeling really hurt because her eyes were dull and dead when she looked at him but her eyes sparkled when she looked at the pretty lady. This was interpreted as, "You have just described your childhood. Your mother's eyes were dull and dead when you were a boy, but her eyes sparkled when you were a girl." After a pause he responded, "That must have been why I always played with dolls."

On occasion Mr. Adams expressed outrage about women dressing in a provocative manner. He was even further outraged that, "Women are allowed to 'get away' with raping infant males by 'forcing' the breast on male infants".

The clinical symptoms that defined Mr. Adams' condition were:
1. Sexual identity confusion
2. Voyeurism
3. Flashing and obscene phone calling.
4. Rage against women
5. Grandiosity

1. Mr. Adams provided numerous associations indicating that, as an infant, he was exposed excessively and traumatically to the female genitalia.

> "Thus, where exposure to the genital organs of another has been early and frequent, the primary incorporation of these precepts may influence identifications and create problems more than when such exposure has taken place largely in the phallic and Oedipal phases. Some degree of fusion of the image of one's own genitals with that of another individual of the same or opposite sex is universal, but the composition of the genital image varies considerably according to the actual experience of exposure." (Rubinfine, 1957, pg. 134)

Excessive and aggressive exposure to the female genitalia had created sexual identity confusion in the mind of the young boy. The penchant of Mr. Adams mother to provide positive reinforcement for 'feminine behavior' and the discounting of his masculine behaviors served as a further blemish to his masculinity.

> "It is in the phallic phase that partial likeness and important differences must be experienced. Elements of the fused genital image must now be rejected and separation of this image from that of objects of the opposite sex must be accomplished." (Rubinfine, 1957 pg. 135)

1. The over-exposure to female genitalia was initially experienced as an unwanted intrusion and a blemish to his masculinity. Mr. Adams succumbed to his mother's exhibitionism.

2. As the first line of defense against the mother's exhibitionism Mr. Adams masochistically submitted to his mother's exhibitionism and transformed his distaste for this behavior into its opposite. Distaste for his mother's exhibitionism was submissively transformed into voyeurism. Voyeurism, as the first line of defense against the intrusive behavior of his mother was experienced as a 'shameful' submission.

3. The second line of defense was against the shame of voyeurism, of masochistic submission to the mother's exhibitionism. This defense (reaction formation) against the shame of voyeurism was the pseudo-aggressive behaviors of flashing and obscene phone calling.

4. The raging against women was also a pseudo-aggressive manifestation of the second line of defense. His perception of the breast being forced on him as being a form of rape had a certain ring, in his own case, of credibility. The supposition that all infant boys were also being 'raped' by having the breast forced on them was an extraordinary case of over-generalization.

5. As the third line of defense against guilt for pseudo-aggressive acts, these acts are chosen for their potential for self-defeat and subsequent punishment. The grandiosity he exhibited on occasion also had its pseudo-aggressive component, as the grandiose plans and pronouncements were essentially self-defeating. Confidentiality does not allow me to report on the punishments comprising his third line of defense.

All the essential components of this case were accessible within the first few interviews. What was not accessible to me initially was the understanding of the essential tripartite nature of the neurotic condition. I feel fortunate that Mr. Adams hung in treatment with me long enough for us both to recognize and accept the essential tripartite or three-layered structure of Mr. Adams' neurotic affliction.

**Neurosis is a three layered defensive structure.**

The first line of defense in the neurotic condition is masochistic submission. The byproduct of this masochistic submission is a sense of shame.

The second line of defense is against the shame of masochistic submission. This defense consists of pseudo-aggressive behaviors. The byproduct of this aggression is guilt.

The third line of defense is against the guilt for aggressive behaviors. As a defense against guilt for aggression, the behaviors chosen as the second line of defense are pseudo-aggressive rather than truly aggressive. These pseudo-aggressive behaviors are chosen because they are essentially self-defeating and subject the neurotic to punishment, punishment that alleviates their sense of guilt.

# Part Four

# PSYCHIC STRUCTURE

The early Bernean formulation for psychic structure was quite easily grasped by beginning and experienced clinicians. An added advantage of these formulations was that the patient also had little difficulty grasping the meaning and understanding of these formulations. Unfortunately some of Berne's followers were somewhat dogmatic in defining the illustrative metaphor of three circles labeled Parent, Adult and Child as things, as a description of all that is needed to define psychic structure.

Berne himself was far more inclusive in this respect. He offered his description of Parent, Adult and Child as metaphor, not as things. I offer only one quote, as an illustration of Berne's more liberal and inclusive perspective.

> "Transactional theory is simpler and more scientifically economical in it's statements than many other psychotherapeutic theories, but its clinical use requires conscientious study, and *in the advanced stages where it begins to overlap with psychoanalytic and existential therapies it takes on increased complexity.* Never the less its principles can be understood and appreciated by any well-trained psychotherapist." *(italics mine)* (Berne, 1966 pg. 216)

There is currently much ferment and foment within the transactional analysis movement pertaining to the topic of structural theory. At present there is much interest and energy devoted to the inclusion of depth in our consideration in the structural theories first presented by Berne some forty years ago.

Part Four is an address to what would seem to be the logical evolution of Bernean ego state theory with the inclusion of the dynamic of depth in the basic ego state diagram. Berne always stated that his ego state diagram should include a third dimension of depth. In these reformulations of transactional analysis ego state theory we are only following the directives first provided by Berne.

# 21

# A Retrospective on States of the Ego

This chapter is divided into two parts. The division is provided because the concept of the objectification of subjective states of experience, and the objectification of observable states of the ego, are concepts seldom addressed and not easily grasped.

To deter my own tendency to objectify the observable state of the ego as experienced by my patients, I find it useful to remind myself that Parent, Adult and Child are not objects. Parent, Adult and Child are metaphor. They are recognizable symbols useful for the purpose of recognizing that the ego entertains at least three distinct and observable conscious experiences of its sense of self.

> "The most fascinating property of language is its capacity to make metaphors. I am using metaphor here in it's most general sense: the use of a term for one thing to describe another because of some kind of similarity between them or between their relations to other things." (Jaynes 1976 pg. 48)

Common examples of metaphor are the head of a company, the face of a cliff, the arm of a chair, the eye of a needle and the tongue of a shoe.

> "What are we trying to do when we try to understand anything? We are trying to find a metaphor for that thing. Not just any metaphor, but one with something more familiar and easy to our attention. Understanding a thing is to arrive at a metaphor for that thing by substituting something more familiar. And the feeling of familiarity is the feeling of understanding." (Jaynes, 1976 pg. 52)

## Part One

At one of the early TA conferences, in referring to a particular incident, someone described in some detail how her Parent, her Adult and her Child had each responded to the incident. I was momentarily taken aback by the need of this individual to demonstrate her grasp of current ego state theory. Upon reflection, I recognized my own opportunistic efforts to demonstrate my own grasp of the current ego state theory. Years later I concluded that my efforts to demonstrate mastery of the theory was a defense against my growing awareness that my understanding of structural theory was simplistic and lacking in depth. This recognition led me first to abandon Bernean ego state theory, and subsequently to a more in-depth re-address to Bernean ego state theory.

Paul Federn called our attention to the fact that the ego may be experienced as subject and object simultaneously. (Federn 1952)

As subject the ego may be known by the pronoun "I," and as object it may be known as "my" feelings, "my" self, "my" Parent, Adult, or Child state of the ego.

The individual described in the previous example did not use the subjective "I." She used the objective "my" Parent, "my" Adult and "my" Child. Her descriptions of her Parent, Adult and Child appeared to be depleted of the ego's identifications with it's own internal objects. The depletion of the ego's identification with it's own objects appeared to have reduced the Parent, Adult and Child states of her ego to objects "out-there," and these states were therefore depleted of their subjective experience of self. Her subjective experience of self had been impoverished.

We need to be aware that the patient is sometimes all too willing to deplete their ego identification with the event as a defense against the subjective experience of a traumatic event, leaving the subjectively experienced emotions of that event free-floating. These free-floating emotions are then subject to transference, displacement and subject to discharge by attaching themselves to current events.

The therapist's task may consist of first assisting the patient to subjectively re-experience the traumatized ego state. The therapist may then facilitate the patient's objectification of the trauma of that state of the ego, depleting the ego's identification with the traumatic event, creating a distance, a breathing space, between the subjective experience and the objective experience of the traumatic event. The objectification of the trauma does not obliterate the trauma. To be sure the trauma will continue to exist in the patient's consciousness, but the objectification of the trauma minimizes the influence the traumatic event will exert on the current and subjective experience of the patient. No longer will the patient have to compulsively re-enact the trauma, or obsessively defend against the possible eruption (displacement) of archaic subjective experiences within the framework of current reality.

Transactional Analysis theory and practice is particularly well suited to the task of objectifying the subjective experience of the patient. The ease with which the interpersonal interaction may be objectively analyzed, utilizing structural and transactional analysis, is a most attractive feature of transactional analysis theory.

This ease may also present a potential hazard. There are situations wherein it may be crucial that the patient re-experience a traumatic event. In these situations there may exist a temptation to objectify and analyze the state, leaving the trauma of that state as a free floating anxiety with the potential to invade and contaminate the patient's subjective experience of current events.

If the therapist, through the use of two-chair gestalt techniques, hypnosis or other regressive techniques, assists the patient to re-experience an archaic and traumatized state of the ego, then that state of the ego may become very much alive in the here and now. The patient then relives the subjective experience of that bygone day. The analysis and identification of the trauma, of the states of the ego that experienced the trauma, and the decisions arrived at in response to the traumatic event allow the patient to objectify, to stand back and objectively look at the traumatic effect of those events. The traumatized state still exists but objectification of the trauma allows the patient to objectify, to distance theirself from the trauma. It provides the patient with the opportunity to form a redecision pertaining to the trauma and the tools to exercise social control and therefore to 'get on with their lives.' (Goulding, 1997)

In 1971 I observed, for the first time, a respected TA therapist's reservations pertaining to the potential for objectifying the experience of observable states of the ego. In the second TA 101 course I attended Dr. Martin Haykin began the course with the original formulation that, "Observable patterns of thinking, feeling and behavior can be defined and interpreted as manifestations of the patient's Parent, Adult or Child ego state."

At the conclusion of the course Dr. Haykin presented later additions to structural theory that were defined as 'advanced structural analysis.' He volunteered that he was not happy with these new formulations but as this was an officially sanctioned transactional analysis training course he was obliged to present these new formulations. The familiar three circles were now labeled as P2, A2 and C2. They had been sliced and diced in interesting ways and objectified to the point where they were beyond the subjective (identifying) experience of anyone.

I silently objected to the reservations voiced by Dr. Haykin. It was only after years of my own contribution to the objectification of ego state theory (Woods, 1981) that I began to experience my own reservations. True, my efforts were useful for the therapist in providing an opportunity to establish an objective view of the role these states of the ego played in the life of the patient. The downside of these efforts was that they were not always useful to the patient. The more I interpreted and modified the basic TA ego state diagram in an effort to analyze states of the ego, the more distant, lifeless, and like an object 'out there' became the subjective experience of these states of the ego. Sometimes this objectification of the ego was useful to the patient. Sometimes it was not.

## Part Two

The objectification of observable states of the ego may mislead the therapist to generalize and form a preconceived concept pertaining to the psychic structure of the patient.

A preconceived concept has its advantages and its disadvantages; it is like a two-edged sword. In the one instance the preconceived concept may allow the clinician to quickly cut to the heart of the problem. In other instances the preconceived concept may cut in the wrong direction.

There is a need to recognize when it is appropriate to address the patient's subjective experience and when it is appropriate to objectify the experience of the patient. To illustrate, the emotions and subjective experience of the addict, either when toxic or in withdrawal, are quite chaotic. The interpretation of the subjective experience of these states is at best, ineffective and short-lived in the experience of the toxic individual.

At its worst, the direct address to the highly unstable and subjectively experienced emotions of this stage may be quite risky.

Some twenty years ago a therapist new to the addiction field attempted to assist a patient in alcohol withdrawal to "get in touch" with his feelings pertaining to his father. The patient rapidly decompensated and had to be hospitalized. Horror stories like this have led the addiction field to look askance at the field of psychotherapy.

The objectification of the subjective experience of these labile emotional states should be the goal of treatment. The program of Alcoholics Anonymous provides the alcoholic with a format that will allow them to order and objectify the chaos of addiction. The AA format provides the alcoholic with Permission, Protection and Potency on a long term and continuous basis. Transactional analysis is also quite adequate to the task of ordering and objectifying these chaotic states. However, preconceived notions pertaining to significant states of the ego may provide their own problems.

A respected transactional analyst had established a successful private practice working primarily with an upwardly mobile and educated clientele. She then contracted to provide training to the staff of a residential treatment facility (RTF) that provided treatment for addiction. Part of that training consisted of conducting treatment sessions for the residents with staff in attendance. In one of the earlier sessions a young man in treatment for addiction described in minute detail the workings of what he defined as his Adult (ego state). The willingness of this young man to work at objectively identifying specific states of the ego was in response to his need to provide 'order' to the chaos of his experience. The feedback the trainer provided was, "That's not how the Adult works." The young man responded, "Lady, that's how *my* Adult works!"

The trainer quickly realized that she could not attribute to this man the problem solving 'style' that was characteristic of her usual clientele. All of this young man's Adult functioning was based on a search for the 'quick fix.' The thinking and problem solving "style" of his ego functioning was characterized by adherence to the pleasure principle, by a primary process mode of problem solving.

Primary process modes of thinking motivate actions in which pleasure is striven for in an imperative, rigid way; and pain is avoided at all costs, even if the avoidance or postponement of present pain will, as a consequence, result in a much more severe and painful subsequent experience of pain. For brevity, the pleasure-pain principle is typically referred to as the "pleasure principle." (Lampl-De Groot (1965)

As an example of the patient abandoning the pleasure principle for the reality principle let us take the case of Mr. Wilkins.

Mr. Wilkins was an athletic, intelligent and capable detainee in a Juvenile Detention Facility. Although he was a pleasant and well liked young man he had managed to spend the bulk of his teenage years locked up. His resentment of authority provided his peers with the means to manipulate him into engaging in pseudo-aggressive and self-defeating activities that he himself recognized as ill advised. When he was placed in a treatment group, he snarled, "Are we supposed to like how it feels?" I responded, "There is a place in our heads that is less interested in how things feel than in how things work." No one had ever told him that before. His ego functioning from that point on was based on the reality principle, on how things work. Mr. Wilkins began holding his head up and combed back his hair. The Cottage Director remarked that it was the first time in years that he had seen Mr. Wilkins' eyes. For the first time, rather than allowing himself to be manipulated by his peers or his own emotions, Mr. Wilkins began to manipulate his environment. He and his best friend, both of whom had been regarded as 'lost causes,' joined together in this endeavor and quickly moved from Level One to Level Three in the cottage. Shortly thereafter Mr. Wilkins was transferred to a less restrictive facility. I later learned that Mr. Wilkins had secured an early release from custody.

Whether the ego functioning of Mr. Wilkins, based on the adoption of the reality principle should be regarded as the birth of a new state of the ego or regarded as an adaptation by the Adult state of his ego of a new mode of functioning remains theoretically unclear. Cases such as this have impressed on me that the diagnosis of an ego state is not always a simple matter.

## Archaic States of the Ego

Some years ago, when transactional analysis was gaining a foothold in our area we started a weekly peer group session for TA therapists. Unfortunately, we did not undertake as our first task to develop a format or group structure. Without a defined goal for the group, without a firm group structure, and without defined group leadership each of us were left to pursue our own personal agendas. Most of us seemed intent on defending and demonstrating our 'expertise.' Any hint of emotion in these sessions, whether positive or negative, was likely to be greeted with the statement, "That is your Child." This confrontational style of relating objectified the other's experience and aborted the person's subjective experience. The group did not address and resolve these issues and so it did not have a very long life.

It is easy to attribute present difficulties to archaic influences when, in fact, they may be a response to current realities. For instance, a patient may enjoy their contact with the therapist. However, this same patient may frequently miss their appointment to engage in more "pleasurable" activities such as getting drunk or getting high or going to bed with someone. If the patient has treatment as a high priority yet skips treatment for a lesser priority, we may be justified in attributing this behavior to an archaic state of the ego. However, if getting someone into bed is the patient's top here-and-now priority, then attributing this behavior to an archaic state of the ego may be in error. Therapists who assume that the patient holds the therapist in higher esteem than reality dictates are prone to this type of error.

# The Influencing Parent

One of my patients reported that whenever he made a mistake, it was if his mother were there in his head and he would hear her saying, "You dummy!" Others have said, "My father would turn over in his grave if I even thought of doing that."

The Influencing Parent is the internalized imago of one's parental figures. This imago will continue to influence the individual's mood and behavior even when the actual parent is deceased or otherwise absent. In my estimation, the Influencing Parent of transactional analysis (Edwards, 1968) and the "psychic presence" as defined by Federn, are one and the same. Weiss (1950) further elaborated Federn's conceptualization of the psychic presence.

> "The term "psychic presence" was selected by the writer to designate the mental image of another ego which, though present only mentally in the ego under observation, affects its emotions and behavior. It is a universal experience that those with whom one holds a relationship of love and affection are represented in one's mind by "living" and reacting images. Such images may be friendly or threatening, consoling or forbidding, in accordance with the emotions attributed to the actual persons. They assume particular vividness when the ego feels that it has violated the interests or expectations of the actual persons represented."
>
> (Weiss, 1950)

In brief, the psychic presence, defined in TA theory as the Influencing Parent, is an intrapsychic event, sometimes inferred but not directly observed by others. Although not directly observable by others this state of the ego does exert an influence on the individual's interactions with others.

# The Active Parent State of the Ego

Transactional Analysis theory postulates that the formation of Parent states of the ego are based on identifications formed with parental figures from our past. The formation of the Influencing Parent is based on *introjection* rather than identification with significant parental figures in our lives. However, theoretically the formation of the Active Parent state of the ego is based on the ego's identification with parental figures.

The Active Parent, according to TA theory, is that state of the ego that on an interpersonal level interacts with others. The Active Parent state of the ego may assume either a critical or a nurturing parental role in its interactions with others.

Transactional analysis theory postulates that the formation of the Critical Parent state of the ego and the Nurturing Parent state of the ego are the product of identifications with significant authority figures from our youth. This theory is simplistic and based on evidence that at best must be defined as slim.

> "When a therapist says, "That is your Parent," a patient will assume the therapist is talking about the Influencing Parent; therapeutic errors can be traced to confusion as to which parent is meant."
>
> (Edwards, 1968 pg. 37)

Parents, other authorities, elected officials or employers will essentially exercise their authority in one of two ways. Either they do *to* others what was done *to* them, or they do *for* others what they would have liked to have had done *for* them.

# The Restrictive Parent

In Scenario One, the child raised in an unduly restrictive evironment may identify with (incorporate) this parental mode and as an adult assume an unduly restrictive stance in relationship with others, doing to others in their exercise of authority, what had been done to them.

In Scenario Two the adult raised in an unduly restrictive environment may not have identified with the restrictive mode of the parental figures. In reaction against their own restrictive upbringing, an archaic state of their own ego may intuitively recognize and identify (resonate) with the ego states of others that feel unduly restricted. They may therefore do for those others that which they would have liked to have had done for themselves under similar circumstances.

In Scenario Three, the adult's parental interactions with others may be based on the Adult's perception of the current reality and also influenced by an archaic state of their own ego's intuitive resonance and identification with the Child state of the ego in others. Identification with parental figures from their own past may or may not provide a major influence.

# The Permissive Parent

In Scenario One, the adult raised by over permissive parents who allowed their children excessive freedom to do whatever they wanted may have identified with (incorporated) this mode of parenting and therefore fail to provide adequate limits for their children.

In Scenario Two, adults raised by over permissive parents who allowed their children excessive freedom to do whatever they wanted, may not have identified with (incorporated) this mode of parenting. As a reaction against over permissive upbringing an archaic state of their own ego may intuitively identify with and resonate with the need in others for a sane structure. As a parent these individuals may provide their own children with the security of the restraints and the limits they so desperately needed during their own childhood.

In Scenario Three the adult's parental interactions with others may be based on the Adult's perception of current reality and also influenced by both an archaic state of their own ego's intuitive resonance with the ego state of another and by identification with (incorporated) parental figures from their own past.

It has been a mistake to theorize that Parent states of the ego are the sole product of identifications with parental figures. Good parenting and perhaps the formation of an Active Parent state of the ego is a combination of considerations of current realities, ego identifications with parental figures from the past and the intuitive response of archaic states of their own ego as they resonate (identify) with similar states in others.

I now conceptualize the Active Parent state of the ego as the Parental rather than the Parent state of the ego.

# 22

# Fascination as a Consequence of the Confluence of Conscious and Unconscious States of the Ego

As teenagers my wife and I were each perplexed by the question of how an entire nation of otherwise educated and civilized people could become fascinated with the person of a sadist like Hitler. As adults both of us became painfully aware of other large groups of individuals that throughout our current history became totally fascinated and submissive to the personage of other leaders such as Jim Jones, Charles Manson, Chuck Diedrick and Saddam Hussein. The widespread fascination with the fictional figure of Dr. Hannibal Lecter also raises the question. What is the secret of their attraction?

Efforts to comprehend this phenomenon only in terms of the personal history and events in the life of the individual are generally unproductive. The evolution of consciousness in the individual mirrors the evolution of the development of consciousness in the collective and in the species. Genetically modern man evolved as a distinct species and arrived on the scene long before the arrival of consciousness. Early man symbolized in his mythology the evolution of the conscious ego from the unconscious.

Consciousness, the recognition that it is *I* who make the decision to undertake a certain course of action and that it is not the Gods or other cosmic forces that initiated this course of action was a late arrival on the human scene.

The early history of the collective is defined by inner primordial images whose projections appeared outside as powerful factors such as gods, spirits, or demons that then became objects of worship.

One symbol of this original perfection is the Great Round. The unity of black and white, night and day, heaven and earth, male and female, Ying and Yang and *good and evil* exists within the Great Round. Within the Great Round nothing comes between good and evil to create duality out of the original unity. In this stage of mankind's evolution:

> "The psyche blends, as does the dream; it spins and weaves together, combining each with each." (Neumann, 1970 pg. 8)

> "This perfect state of being, in which the opposites are contained, is perfect because it is autarchic. Its self-suffi-ciency, self-contentment, and independence of any "you" and any "other" are signs of its self-contained eternality"

> (Neumann, 1970 pg. 9)

Berne advanced ego state theory significantly when he differentiated the conscious ego into Parent, Adult and Child states of the ego. He fur-ther stated that the two dimensional diagram of three circles signifying

Parent, Adult and Child states of the ego should really be a three dimensional diagram.

Let us take as an example the process of learning to drive a car. In this process we are consciously aware of each of the steps we are going through. We remain consciously aware that we are now putting our foot down on the clutch and that we are now shifting gears. Our conscious ego will be fully aware of each step we take in driving the car from point A to point B. With practice and the development of skill we begin to accomplish these tasks without conscious awareness of having engaged in the necessary steps. We may drive from point A to point B on automatic pilot. So what has happened to the conscious state of the ego that formerly drove the car? That formerly conscious state of the ego has been *supplanted* by a later conscious state of the ego. The formerly conscious state of the ego is now an unconscious state of the ego. This state of the ego might now be conceptualized as residing in a third dimension of the Bernean ego state diagram. The proof of the continued existence of this state of the ego resides in the fact that even when our conscious mind is distracted the unconscious state of the ego will continue to drive the car. Conscious states of the ego may be metaphorically identified as Parent, Adult and Child states of the ego. We need to remain cognizant of the fact that currently observable, conscious and subjectively experienced states of the ego are states of the ego that have supplanted previous Parent, Adult and Child states of the ego. The supplanted and previously conscious states of the ego are now *unconscious* states of the ego. They reside within what Berne defined as the third dimension of the ego state diagram. These unconscious states of the ego may or may not influence or contaminate a conscious state of the ego.

Eric Berne first achieved recognition for his work with compensated or stabilized schizophrenics. Utilizing the familiar three circles signifying conscious Parent, Adult and Child states of the ego Berne was able to assist these patients in establishing social control. However, when the patient is in the grips of a psychotic episode the therapist will be unable to make contact with conscious Parent, Adult or Child states of the ego. Therefore this approach may not be appropriate in addressing a psychotic episode.

## Direct Analysis

The methodology utilized by John Rosen for addressing the psychotic state was defined as Direct Analysis because Rosen worked directly with the unconscious ego of his patients. His patients were living in the experience of the psychosis as though it was just happening to them and they were unaware of any conscious will of their own. Their unconscious had opened up and they had literally fallen into the unconscious. Conscious and observable Parent, Adult and Child states of the ego were not in evidence. They could not make a conscious attempt to discover the meaning of their experience since conscious states of the ego were simply not available. They were unable to accept that acts were of their own volition.

I had the privilege of viewing a twenty-minute tape of John Rosen demonstrating of his work with a patient he had never seen before. When Rosen asked the patient why he was in the hospital the patient replied, "It's the rays." Just as early man was unconscious of his own will or volition this patient was unconscious of any choice in his actions. *It was the rays.* In short, the patient was operating from an unconscious rather than a conscious state of his ego. Rosen responded to the patient by saying, "Oh! I know all about rays!" He then asked the patient, "What kind of rays are they? Are they the kind that came down from above or are they the ones that come up from below?" Rosen then went on to discuss radio waves and how they were rays and they carry messages and that most people just didn't understand about rays. This almost-mute patient responded to Rosen's honoring and recognition of his unconscious perception by providing a wealth of information about his history that the

hospital had been unable to gather during the months of his hospitalization. Rosen then responded to the patient's unconscious perception
of being at the mercy of the rays by telling the patient that he loved him
and that he would protect him. Rosen then asked the patient to look
into his eyes. The patient visibly struggled but was unable to look John
Rosen in the eye. The patient was returned to the ward and discussion
of the demonstration followed. Rosen stated, 'If you want to talk to this
man then you are going to have to go where he's at. If you don't want to
talk to him continue to fill him full of drugs." Rosen then said, "You
notice he could not look me in the eye. If he had looked me in the eye it
would have been all over."

My own perception of the demonstration was that John Rosen first
went to where the patient was at and joined the patient in his unconscious
perception of reality. Having established contact with the unconscious of
the patient and having reassured some of the anxieties residing in his
unconscious Rosen then appealed to the patient to join him in consciousness. It seemed to me that it was only with great effort that the patient was
able to avoid joining John Rosen in conscious reality.

## Fascination

There resides within the unconscious that early state of the ego that
saw the world and those in it as contained within the Great Round as
symbolized in mythology. This round is sometimes symbolized as an
image of a snake eating its own tail. This round contains the All. The All
includes the good and the bad, life and death, the Great Mother and the
Great Father. Within this unconscious state of the ego there is no duality or separation of the Great Mother from the Great Father. Great
Mother/Great Father beckon to take consciousness back into the
unconsciousness. Always over this beckoning stands the symbol of
death, signifying final dissolution of the conscious self.

However much the world forced early man, and for that matter the child in modern times to face reality, it is with great reluctance that the child enters into this reality. Modern man may be confronted with a conscious and dualistic image of a grand parental figure that holds the potential of great nurturing and support as well *as the potential for cruelty and death.* The conscious state of the ego that recognizes the leader's potential for nurturing and support may also recognize that union with the leader may lead to cruelty and the death of their own conscious volition *as well as to life itself.* The conscious state of the ego may therefore experience a realistic fear pertaining to the leader.

An early and now unconscious state of the ego may refute this fear and refute this dualism of the leader. The unconscious may desire a reunion with the image of the Great Mother/Great Father. This unconscious state of the ego may contaminate the conscious perception of this realistic danger to the extent that conscious fear is supplanted. The unconscious may *contaminate* our conscious perception of the danger to the extent that our realistic perception and conscious perception of danger is defensively transformed into fascination. The conscious ego then becomes passive in relation to the leader. The fascination with the leader will become a component of our conscious ego and the formerly realistic judgement pertaining to the objective reality of their relationship with the leader becomes lost.

## In Conclusion

Transactional Analysis was initially formulated and defined by Berne as a social psychiatry.

However, from the very beginning Berne left intriguing hints of how further development of transactional analysis might proceed in the direction of inclusions of a depth psychology. His reference to the ego state diagram as it should include a third dimension defining depth is quite clear. Berne further stated:

> "Every human being seems to have a small fascist in his head. This is derived from the deepest layers of the personality. In civilized people it is usually deeply buried beneath a platform of social ideals and training."
>
> (Berne 1972 pg. 268)

Berne also stated (1972 pg. 269) that as the human embryo grows it relives the whole evolutionary tree and that the child relives the prehistory of the human race. It would appear that prior to his death in 1970 Berne may have postulated or envisioned the possible inclusion of a depth psychology in the future evolution of transactional analysis.

Edmund Bergler stated that psychic masochism is the basic neurosis that mankind is heir to. It would appear that Bergler was correct.

In a previous article we have addressed the transactional and the interpersonal aspects of psychic masochism. In this chapter I have attempted to define psychic masochism, the fascination with the sadistic other, as it is recorded within the conscious and unconscious states of the ego. It is an unconscious state of the ego *residing within us all* that provides the structural basis for the widespread incidence of manic defenses as is exemplified in our societies fascination with the character of a Hannibal Lecter.

# 23

# Freud's Contribution to the Concept of the Natural Child

Over the past thirty years I have experienced difficulty accepting the usual conceptualization of the Natural Child state of the ego. Attendance at various functions wherein individuals would be jumping around and otherwise attempting to demonstrate that they were in touch with their own Natural Child were unconvincing. These behaviors appeared to be new adaptations pertaining to a new social setting.

## Example One

*At one of these functions a woman who was quietly sitting was encouraged to, "Come on! Let your kid out!" With poise and confidence this lady replied, "My little girl is out. She is very quiet." This lady grew up in a highly verbal, educated professional family setting. In her more usual mode of behavior she was known to be articulate, exuberant and witty.*

I would question whether we should identify either her articulate and witty self or her quiet and observing self as a manifestation of the

Natural Child. Each of these sets of observable behaviors may be an example of separate and distinct adjustments or adaptations that the child chose in response to specific and distinct social pressures.

It is an axiom of TA ego state theory that ego states are observable phenomenon yet we retain the reservation that, "All that we see is not all that there is."

## Example Two

A gentleman of my acquaintance, after completing a long prison term, successfully founded a residential drug treatment facility. The first six months of his long sentence had been served in solitary confinement. He had killed a woman over seventeen cents. During the period when I was acquainted with this man he attended a Lifespring workshop in which the participants were encouraged to jump around and otherwise "get into their child." He said, "I'm not going to do it! I've been a clown all my life and I'm not going to do it!" This was a gentleman that others would not be too inclined to argue with. The question is how should we define these manifestations of sets of behavior? Should the clowning be classified as a manifestation of the Natural Child or the killing of a woman over seventeen cents be defined as a manifestation of the Natural Child?

> "The adapted Child is an archaic ego state which is under the Parental influence, while the Natural Child is an archaic ego state which is free from or is attempting to free itself from such influence." ( Berne, pg. 25, 1961)

The socialized child is never free of the parental influence. If they were totally free of a parental influence, he or she would not be a social being.

After having been transactional analyzed, psychoanalyzed, gestalted and psycho-dramaed, I can only state that my own Influencing Parent and Natural Child state of the ego had remained largely unobserved and unrecognized. I had only observed what I believe has been their influence pertaining to my behavior.

That state of the ego metaphorically defined as the Adapted Child state of the ego is characterized by the "I must," while that state of the ego metaphorically defined as the Natural Child state of the ego is characterized by the "I wish." Since the child denies a substantial portion of their own wishes in order to get along in the world it would appear the Natural Child state of the ego may not be directly observable. We may infer, however, that the repressed wishes of the Natural Child do exert an unforeseen influence on observable patterns of behavior.

After reading "Freud, A Life for Our Times" (Gay 1988) I was teased by the report that during a period when the psychoanalytic movement was debating whether it should certify lay analysts, Freud stated that anyone who conducts their own dream analysis is in essence a psychoanalyst. To test the validity of this statement I decided to undertake my own dream analysis within analytic parameters as defined by Freud. As I reviewed Freud's analyses of his own dreams I had difficulty with comprehending how Freud's associations to the manifest content of the dream could possibly have provided the means to arrive at a valid interpretation and understanding of the dream. How the associations, as described in Freud's reports of his dream analyses, could have found their way to the latent content and the wish fulfillment of the dream seemed almost magical and obviously beyond the scope of those of us who lacked the genius of a Freud. However, when I began analyzing my own dreams I found that free associating to each of the manifest components of my dreams easily and inevitably revealed the latent content of the dream. Evidently when the dreamer is willing to see the path is not hard to find.

These recently undertaken analyses of my own dreams have provided me with the pleasing discovery that Freudian dream theory and Transactional Analysis ego state theory are more compatible than I would have suspected.

## First Dream

I dreamed I was writing an article on my computer when there was a loud and insistent knocking on the glass windows of both of the doors to my house. Both doors were locked. They were not trying to get in but their knocking was irritating and distracting. I became enraged and looked for a weapon. The only thing within reach was a plastic coat hanger. I grabbed the coat hanger and rushed out the nearest door and chased the one banging on the front door around to the back door where I cornered him. He was bigger than I, well over six feet and muscular. He had a blond crewcut. Despite his size and muscular build I had little trouble punching him out. Then the other one showed up. He was smaller than I, with dark hair and exhibited a pleasant and friendly manner. He appeared unsure as to what he was supposed to do. I punched him out as well. We then affected a reconciliation in which we all shook hands with each other and both men agreed not to disturb me anymore by knocking on my window. In my dream we parted on friendly terms.

Associations to the elements of the manifest dream were, "The larger man looked German. Freud spoke German and his oedipal theories had been on my mind lately.

Associations to Freud and his authority pointed to parental figures that had successfully persuaded me to discontinue going to school. Later, these same parental figures persuaded me that I did not have a future at my then present job. After leaving this job reliable sources informed me that I had actually been the one in line for the promotion that would have put me on an "upwardly mobile path."

Associations to the younger man were that he appeared to be over-compliant and controlled by the authority of the larger man. He apparently had no personal investment in disturbing me but had reluctantly complied with a directive from the larger man. In the dream I was not angry with him, but never the less felt that he needed to be punched out. I associated the younger man in my dream with myself in my younger years when I had allowed myself to be manipulated into undertaking actions that proved disastrous. Associations to the plastic coat hanger were that a plastic coat hanger is not a very good weapon. What you can do with a coat hanger is hang your coat on it and get back to work, which on second thought is a pretty good weapon.

I had difficulty identifying any association to the locked doors. I therefore turned to symbolism. Doors and other openings often symbolize openings in the body. Apparently, the locked doors symbolized my caution, my decision to be careful and guard against allowing myself to get screwed again.

Freud stated that the latent content of each dream contains a wish fulfillment. The wish fulfillment of this dream was the punching out of parental figures that had screwed me over.

In James Strachey's translation of Freud's 1952 book "On Dreams" he defined the wish that motivates the dream as an optative clause. The dream represents the Natural Child's denied wishes as fulfilled in the present. The optative clause is the dream wish expressed as an "if only!" The optative clause (Freud, 1952 pg. 39) defines the concerns of the Natural Child state of the ego *in the early history of the dreamer.* The "If only" of this dream is, "If only I had punched them out they would have left me alone." This understandable wish of the Natural Child had been denied to the point that I had remained unaware of this wish for over fifty years.

Freudian dream theory states that the associations to the manifest dream elements will lead us to the optative clause, the repressed and unfulfilled childhood wishes of the dreamer, the denied wishes fulfilled within the latent content of the dream. In transactional analysis terms, a thorough Freudian dream analysis will reveal the unconscious wishes of the Natural Child state of the ego.

## Second Dream

I woke up early from a confused and unintelligible dream I had every intention of writing down and analyzing. I drifted off to sleep again and had another dream, woke up remembering this dream but had forgotten the previous dream. I repeated this scenario three times. I awoke from the fourth dream and stayed awake. I remembered nothing of the first three dreams. This is the manifest content of the fourth dream.

"I was gift wrapping four packages. The packages were about nine inches long and two inches wide and deep. I was tying a ribbon around the fourth package. An onlooker came by and responded with derisive laughter to my putting a ribbon on the fourth package. I also was laughing with derisive humor pertaining to this undertaking."

Associations to the four packages were that they appeared to be phallic symbols. The bow reminded me that I had recently heard a report of a man who tied a ribbon to his penis before flashing it. Why four packages? The associations to the number four were that I had one father and three stepfathers. Why the ribbon on just the fourth package? The final stepfather had been particularly destructive. The associations to gift giving were that I experience a compulsive need to write clinical articles and otherwise exhibit my potency. The four packages to four parental figures were to demonstrate that I still had my potency. The latent-content and wish fulfillment of this dream is that four parental figures would be confronted with my potency. It was the unconscious and long denied wish to "flash" my potency that provided the impetus for this dream.

Analysis of this short dream provided me with the understanding of why the first draft of each of my articles has always exhibited a belligerent tone requiring moderating in subsequent drafts.

## Third Dream

I dreamed that my mother and I had attended an event at an airport terminal in Montana. In the dream I left the terminal walking and took a shortcut across a muddy field to my mother's house some distance away. I then began to think about how I was going to get my mother to her home. A passenger plane rolled up to my mother's house with my mother sitting in the cockpit with the pilot. The pilot was named Ned. He was very friendly and stated that he had recognized us at the terminal and therefore had given my mother a ride home. Ned and the plane then rolled away. My mother and I were sure that Ned knew us but we could not remember ever meeting him. Ned had promised to pick us up in the morning and fly us to Seattle. Eddy was a childhood friend. He and his wife had come to the event and were walking on the highway on the way back to Seattle. I hurried down the highway to catch up to Eddy and his wife. When I caught up with them I saw that they were shorter and sturdier built than I remembered. They looked tired, having walked all the way from Seattle and were now determined to endure the walk all the way back under their own power. I pompously stated that I didn't need to do that anymore and that I now knew where to get help for where I needed go. I admired their determination to reach their destination without help from anyone while at the same time I was contemptuous of my own position of having found an easier way.

The manifest content of this dream was derived from the residue of the previous evening. On the previous evening my wife and I were on our way to a New Years Eve party when the car broke down. I had to walk some distance and phone a friend who left the party to come and pick up my wife and myself.

My associations to the material of this dream started with Eddy. Eddy was my best friend from my latency years. Associations to this period were that this was the period when I moved with my mother from Portland to Seattle. The trip of less than two hundred miles took two days because we were being driven by a drunk who had to stop at every tavern along the way. I think that I must have prayed to have someone come down from the sky and rescue us from that trip. It was shortly after our move to Seattle that I became a devout atheist. Associations to the shortcut across a muddy field reminded me of the move from Seattle to Montana in my sixteenth year. The driver on that trip saw on the map what appeared to him to be a shortcut to our destination. We became stuck in the mud on this back-road and I walked miles in the dark to find someone to pull us out of the mud. Associations to my mother arriving home in the cockpit of a passenger plane with Ned as the pilot were that someone from out of the sky had rescued us. The pilot named Ned was also going to fly us to Seattle in the morning. My associations to the name of Ned led to my recent viewing of the film "The Waking of Ned Devine." In this film Ned Devine, though dead, had held the winning lottery ticket in his hand. Though dead, Ned had 'rescued' the small village where he lived. It was my Natural Child's denial of the wish for someone from out of the sky to come down and rescue us that had killed God and led to my conversion to atheism. My admiration for Eddy and his wife's determination to go it alone and my contempt for my own response of having found an easier way were a further attempt to maintain the denial of my Natural Child's wish to be rescued.

It is only when I have conducted a free association to each of the individual components of the manifest dream that I have arrived at a useful interpretation of the denied wishes of the Natural Child.

I have been tempted to shortcut the dream analysis process by free associations to the dream scenario in its entirety. My efforts to find the meaning of a dream by associations to the manifest content of the dream as a whole has led me only to seemingly plausible but lifeless and useless interpretations of the dream.

It would appear that the manifest content of the dream is arranged in a manner to mislead and maintain the denial of the wishes of the Natural Child.

## In Summary

In those cases where the dreamer is knowledgeable pertaining to TA ego state theory, this knowledge may act as day residue in the formation of the manifest content of the dream. This is particularly evident in the first dream reported in this series. Analysis of dreams along Freudian lines will reveal that even within a dream whose manifest content is quite unpleasant, hidden within the latent content of the dream is the optative clause. The latent content of the dream will express the fulfillment of the long denied wishes of the Natural Child state of the ego.

Freud defined dream analysis as the royal road to the unconscious. As a TA therapist I would reinterpret Freud's definition to the effect that for the transactional analyst, dream analysis along Freudian lines is the royal road to the recognition of the long denied wishes of the Natural Child.

# 24

# The Natural Child Re-Evaluated

This chapter will address what I now perceive as my early misperception pertaining to what is true in the concept of a Natural Child state of the ego. Also I will address what I believe to be the neglect and lack of recognition of the importance of Berne's conceptualization of a Natural Child state of the ego.

At one of the TA seminars in the late seventies Pat Jarvis, presented us with a question to ponder. "Which is the most important, a theory that works or a theory that is true?" He then stated that the theory that works is the most important. However, he then stated that when what is supposed to work doesn't work then we have to determine what is true.

## What is Important

My early theoretical understanding of transactional analysis resulted in a tendency to address and recognize only phenomenological realities, i.e. observable Parent, Adult and Child states of the ego. I tended to negate or deny not only the influence but also the existence of latent and not directly observable Parent or Child states of the ego. I embraced the commonly espoused belief that ego states were 'things' and were therefore directly observable. To free the Adapted Child of parental prohibitions became my goal. Actually, this theoretical approach worked very well in my work with those individuals frequently identified as those whose lifestyle reflected a restricted and over-adapted upbringing. However, this theoretical approach in my work with individuals who seemed to lack self-restraint, i.e. some personality disorders, didn't work very well. Since the theory wasn't working with these individuals it became necessary to abandon a theory that didn't work. It became necessary to search for what was true.

## What is True

My early theoretical understanding failed to account for the fact that the Natural Child state of the ego also has a dark side. Berne briefly addressed the topic of the dark side of the Natural Child state of the ego when he wrote about "The Little Fascist."

> "Every human being seems to have a small fascist in his head. This is derived from the deepest layers of the personality (the Child in the Child). In civilized people *it is usually deeply buried beneath a platform of social ideals and training.*"
>
> (Berne, 1971 pg. 268) *italics mine*

I contend that 'The Little Fascist' as defined by Berne represents the dark side of the Natural Child state of the ego. Berne seems to indicate that the influence of the small fascist may be inferred even though this state of the ego is not directly observable. It is buried beneath a layer of social adaptation. In other words we could say that the little fascist is the dark side of the Natural Child state of the ego. Under normal conditions the Natural Child state of the ego is denied as the child adapts to the social reality.

As I review the original transactional analysis treatise, "Transactional Analysis in Psychotherapy" (Berne 1961) I find little indication that Berne conceptualized ego states as "things." To quote from the initial paragraph in the Introduction to this seminal work:

> "An ego state may be described phenomenological as a coherent system of feelings related to a given subject, and operationally as a set of coherent behavior patterns; or pragmatically, as a system of feelings which motivates a related set of behavior patterns." (Berne 1961 pg. xvii)

I have for some time held that there is only one ego and that the ego has and is currently undergoing varied states of experience. Possibly, it may have been the prevalence of the term ego state that could have misled me to conceptualize differing states of the ego as distinct and separate egos. Utilizing the term 'states of the ego' allows the recognition of 'states' as differing aspects of an intact ego.

The Natural Child state of the ego is comprised of those wishes, feelings and impulses that the child in the process of its maturation and socialization has been forced to deny. It is the child's identification with the collective social norms that provides the formation of the socialized and Adapted Child state of the ego. This process of adaptation and socialization supplants those emotions and wishes that motivate the Natural Child state of the ego.

> "The Adapted Child is an archaic ego state which is under the parental influence, while the Natural Child is

an archaic ego state which is free from or is attempting
to free itself from such influence."

(Berne, 1961 pg. 25)

As stated in the previous chapter formal dream analysis conducted
along Freudian lines will reveal the unconscious wishes of the Natural
Child state of the ego. Recognition of the unconscious wishes of the
Natural Child provides us with an awareness of how these unconscious
and latent wishes may intrude themselves and influence the current
behavior of active and observable states of the ego. Although Freud's
contribution preceded that of Berne, I would define Freudian dream
analysis proper as a major contribution to Bernean ego state theory. A
properly conducted Freudian dream analysis will reveal the unconscious and denied wishes of the Natural Child state of the ego. Such
revelations are not always pleasant or comfortable as they sometimes
reveal an unsuspected 'dark side' of the Natural Child.

Berne (1961 pg. 62) informs us that the intrusion of a single element
or a set of elements from a latent ego state into an active one should
bear the characteristics of the intruding ego state.

When I attended the 1999 TA Summer Conference in San Francisco I
was informed that strenuous efforts were still being undertaken to catalog the specific and observable characteristics of specific and active
states of the ego. Efforts to catalog the characteristics of active states of
the ego would need to consider the influence of latent (Influencing
Parent and Natural Child) intrusions as they are incorporated in each
case. These latent states of the ego do influence the functioning of
currently active and observable states of the ego. I would suggest that
possibly the examination of social movements might more easily lend
itself to such an undertaking. All of the social unrest of the sixties, the
anti-war movement, the beatniks, the flower children and emergence of
violent anti-government and white-supremacist groups were broadly
generalized by some observers as examples of what they defined as an

adolescent rebellion against what was perceived as an oppressive and impersonal authority.

In Greek history it was the rebellion against an oppressive matriarchy that ushered in the 'golden age' of Greek art, philosophy and poetry. The dark side of this rebellion was that pederasty also became an accepted norm.

Transactional Analysis evolved in the sixties as a rebellion against the oppressive authority of psychoanalysis. This rebellion against the authority of psychoanalysis provided transactional analysis with it's own 'golden age' of creativity in which a host of creative new concepts came to the front. The dark side of this rebellion was that sadistic practices such as game confrontation as opposed to game interpretation, and the acceptance of abusive practices such as face slapping and corporal punishment also became accepted as appropriate to the treatment of psychotic patients.

There are therapists who have had great success utilizing the concept of an Adolescent state of the ego as a separate entity. This is important. What is true is that the adolescent rebellion is the result of an intrusion into the Adult by an archaic (Natural Child) state of the ego. I would caution that this intrusion could contain not only creativity and spontaneity but also the dark side of the Natural Child state of the ego.

"At present it seems best to treat "the adolescent" as a structural problem rather than as a separate entity or ego state *sui generis*." (Berne, 1961 pg. 71)

> "The Child means an organized state of the mind which exists or once actually existed, while Freud describes the id as a chaos, a cauldron of seething excitement. It has no organization and no unified will."
>
> (Berne, 1961 pg. 48-49)

Dream analysis and other methods of investigation reveal that the Natural Child state of the ego is well organized and does have a unified will. Fairbairn (1952/1996) may have been the first within the psychoanalytic fold to state that the child is born with an intact rudimentary ego, that there is no id and therefore there can be no death instinct or life instinct. Berne's conceptualization of the Natural Child state of the ego supersedes and makes unnecessary the Freudian conceptualization of the id. The importance of Berne's recognition of the Natural Child state of the ego has, in my opinion, not received the attention it merits.

Whether the Natural Child state of the ego manifests it's influence within autonomous forms of behavior such as rebelliousness or self-indulgence, or whether the unconscious wishes of the Natural Child are revealed by a properly conducted dream analysis, one thing remains clear. The Natural Child state of the ego is well-organized, is not all sweetness and light as many would like to believe and definitely has a will of it's own.

It is the intrusion of the therapist's unanalyzed and unrecognized dark side of his or her Natural Child state of the ego that allows them to justify and engage in unethical and harmful treatment procedures. An analysis of the dark side of the candidate's Natural Child state of the ego would seem to be a consideration in the training and certification of the clinician.

# 25

# Passion, the Natural Child and the Hot Potato

It is passion, not instinct, that motivates the Natural Child state of the ego. It is the relative expression, denial, suppression or sublimation of these passions that will foment the formation of character.

Whereas animals may be driven by their instincts to travel in great migratory journeys or travel back to the place of their birth to spawn and die, man is driven, not by instinct, but by their characterological passions. Character, according to Fromm, 1973, is man's "second nature," the substitute for his poorly developed instincts. Man's character-conditioned passions are an answer to his existential needs and they are specifically human.

> "To give an example: man can be driven by love or the passion to destroy: in each case he satisfies one of his existential needs: the need to "affect," or to move something, to "make a dent." (Fromm, 1973 pg. 26)

The Freudian position that man is driven by the sexual instinct is no longer tenable. Man is driven by his passions and these passions are seldom of a sexual nature. These passions are the precursor to his definable character. It is important that we recognized the distinction between 'organic drives' for food, fight, flight and sexuality that are frequently referred to as 'instincts' whose function it is to preserve the individual and the species,' and the non-organic drives,' the character-rooted passions.

A passion for life and progress would appear to be more prominent in our society than a passion for death and destruction. Headlines sometimes report extraordinary cases of individuals who have passionately pursued a long course of serial murder. In the aftermath of these events too much attention is devoted to what may have been the external factors that may have triggered the individuals course of action. Too little if any attention has been given to addressing the individual's passion for death and destruction, a passion and interest that usually has been clearly evident since the child's earliest years.

I would repeat that man is not a slave to his instincts but that he or she develops passions in response to their existential needs. In retrospect I now recognize several cases wherein I failed to recognize and address the patient's necrotus character structure, the passion for death and destruction. It was my failure to address this passion for death and destruction that led to the destruction and death of the therapeutic relationship.

Sadistic, masochistic, narcissistic, necrotus as well as the oral, anal and phallic characters are driven by their passion, not their instinct, to satisfy their existential needs.

For some the sublimation of negative passions into related activities may provide fruitful, happy and productive lifestyle. For instance, the sublimation of a passion for voyeurism could provide the basis for a productive career as a therapist. Possibly others (though we cannot be sure of this) may have denied certain negative passions to the extent that they are not a factor in their life.

Positive characterological developments in response to the passions of the Natural Child state of the ego, though interesting and heartening, are not the topic of this article.

The passions of some individuals may be reactively transformed into its opposite. They become defensively transformed into a reaction formation against those very passions in others.

## Example One

As a defense against his sadistic passions a police officer developed a reaction formation against his own sadism and energetically pursued others who engaged in sadistic behaviors. However, his children could not help recognizing his vicarious pleasure in his recounting of the offender's crimes. This recognition, in at least one of his children, acted as a hot potato (English, 1969) fostering and nurturing the sadistic passions of the child. The father's subsequent vicarious enjoyment of his offspring's exercise of power over others and his approval of their passion for meting out punishment reinforced the sadistic passions of his offspring.

## Example Two

As a defense against their passions pertaining to behaviors considered in polite society as immoral, a married evangelical missionary couple mounted a moral crusade against 'sin.' This hotbed of references to sin was quite titillating for their only child. The passions stirred up by these references to 'sin' were denied well into adulthood and were released only upon entering therapy. This individual's therapist lamented to me that, "I cured her of a neurotic condition, freed her from her parental adaptation and unleashed a psychopathy."

I would submit at this time that we give some consideration to the patient's character structure, to those passions residing within the

Natural Child state of the patient's ego, as we plan our address to the patient's presenting difficulties. Adaptation is not always bad.

# Example Three

Two rather dramatic enactments of what Berne (1972) defined as the "Little Red Riding Hood" script are the topic of Example Three. It is the 'passions' residing within the Natural Child state of the ego's of the mothers of our two 'Little Red Riding Hoods' that triggered these two script enactments.

# Enactment One

A married couple came seeking treatment. The wife was wearing a red cape and was sporting a black eye. The couple had recently returned from a three-day retreat/workshop. The couple had shared one small bedroom with the wife's mother, who had financed the couple's attendance at the retreat. On the second night of the retreat the wife and a co-therapist secured a key and disappeared into the library. The husband figured out where they might be. When they came out of the darkened library the husband was waiting and punched his wife in the eye. For the moment, the husband had stepped out of his usual role as the Honest Woodsman and instead of hitting the wolf, hit his wife. At the beginning of the couples third appointment the wife dramatically announced, "I was raped last night." The husband, in a voice filled with boredom said, "Again." Neither the wife nor her mother had ever learned to drive. On a regular basis the wife hitchhiked some distance to and from her mother's home. Standing pigeon-toed and looking vulnerable these trips often resulted in reports of having been raped. The mother regularly encouraged her daughter to engage in these dangerous trips. What stands out most clearly to me in this case is that the mother demanded that her daughter, the Little Red Riding Hood of our case, always report to her mother every single detail of her sexual escapades. Although the mother had been celibate for many years the Natural Child state of her ego had a vicarious interest in the sexual activity of others. It was the voyeuristic passions of the mother's Natural state of her ego that had scripted her daughter to play out the role of a Little Red Riding Hood. The husband finally had enough and dissolved the marriage. Shortly thereafter the ex-wife's mother died. After her mother's death I saw the daughter on two occasions. On those two occasions the coquettish Little Red Riding Hood of the past was no more. The former Little Red Riding Hood had been reduced to a dull and drab individual who elicited little attention.

## Enactment Two

In this case the role of Little Red Riding Hood was enacted by a 14 year old boy. The role of the Big Bad Wolf was enacted by a 36 year old man. The boy's mother had sent him on an errand to the home of the Big Bad Wolf and the boy had compliantly climbed into bed with the big Bad Wolf. The mother knew that the Big Bad Wolf of our account was quite unstable. The boy had a previous history of being sexually abused. This raises the question, "Why did the mother send her child off alone to the home of the Big Bad Wolf and why did the boy compliantly get into the Wolf's bed?"

During the ensuing Court proceedings it became apparent that the boy cast in the role of Little Red Riding Hood was not the central character in this drama; his presence was "not required" through most of the proceedings and considerations pertaining to his subsequent welfare were little more than afterthoughts.

Without being accused the mother in this case volunteered that she was not an absentee mother. She stated that she wouldn't even leave her son with baby sitters when he was little because he had previously been sexually abused, *just as she had.* She further Reported that the defendant, the Big Bad Wolf, had been her very best friend for seven years. Why did the mother choose as her very best friend the Defendant? He was obviously perverse and unstable. Also, why did she sanction and encourage contact between the Defendant and her son? Her testimony in Court was quite animated and she appeared to derive great pleasure from the Defendant's predicament. During a break in the proceedings and when passing the Defendant and his attorney in the hallway the mother laughed and said, "Have fun you guys!"

When Court was resumed the mother stated, "I trusted the Defendant with my son and *I want justice!*"

The passion that dominated the mother's Natural Child state of the ego was a *passion for revenge* relating to the sexual abuse that had been her lot as a child. She was seeking revenge not *for* her son but *through her son,* for the sexual abuse that she herself had suffered.

Bern's description of the Hunter in the story of Little Red Riding Hood is worth considering.

> "The Hunter is obviously a rescuer who enjoys working over his vanquished opponents with sweet little maidens to help: quite obviously an adolescent script."
>
> (Berne, 1972 pg. 44)

In response to the mother's plea the Judge assumed the role of the Hunter. He stated, "The victim often does not feel as though they have received justice *(he related to her as though she, not her son, were the victim),* and the parameters of the law place limits on how much time the Defendant can be sentenced for a given offense." He then sentenced the Defendant to the maximum sentence allowable by law.

It was clear that the Judge's sentence was handed down to satisfy the mother's passion for revenge in relationship to her own sexual abuse.

Her son had been all but forgotten. Berne (1972 pg. 44) states that the moral of the story of Little Red Riding Hood is not that maidens should keep out of forests where there are wolves, but that wolves should keep away from innocent-looking maidens. A wolf should not walk through the forest alone.

# 26

# Intuition, Cognition and Ego Structure

The formal training I received in transactional analysis neglected to address Berne's detailed and fascinating studies of the intuitive process. Intuition was defined as the province of the Little Professor, the Adult in the Child. That was the sum total of the attention given to the intuitive process in my early training.

The connection between Berne's studies of the intuitive process and his subsequent formulations of transactional analysis and structural analysis appear as somewhat oblique rather than direct. The formula he provided pertaining to the intuitive process stated that the primal image precedes the primal judgment and that the primal judgment precedes the intuition. *Under normal conditions the primal image and the primal judgment are retained in an unconscious or preconscious state.* (Berne, 1977)

Primal Image-> Primal Judgment-> Intuition

This formulation, though useful, is devoid of considerations pertaining to either the cognitive process or to ego state theory. In his last article on the intuitive process, first published in 1962, Berne provided a more direct though perfunctory connection between intuition as it pertained to his ego state theory. (Berne, 1977)

This article is undertaken to provide a more direct connection between cognition as it pertains to the intuitive process, and ego state theory as it pertains to the intuitive process.

> "A primal image is the image of an infantile object relation-ship; that is, of the use of the function of an erogenous zone for social expression. A primal judgment is the understanding (correct or incorrect) of the potentialities of the object relationship represented by the image. In the normal adult, under ordinary conditions, neither the primal image nor the primal judgment comes into awareness. Instead, a more or less distant derivative, which is called here an intuition, may become conscious." (Berne, pg. 67, 1977)

> "Primal judgments imply an understanding, based on such images, of certain archaic unconscious attitudes of other people. These attitudes are derived from early instinctual vicissitudes and express a deep and persistent infantile quality in object relationships."
>
> (Berne, pg. 67, 1977)

> "Primal judgments give rise to part of the emotional substance of everyday life. This is most apparent in the encounters with strangers. New acquaintances may be characterized in vulgar gossip as pricks, jerks, assholes, farts, stinkers, shits, suckers, or bitches, sluts, pushovers, cock teasers, cats, bleeding hearts, clotheshorses. All these opprobrious terms are intuitive derivatives of

primal images. The images themselves can easily be elicited by free association to any of the epithets."

(Berne, 1977 pg. 81)

The therapist, upon boarding a train, was forced to pass a fellow passenger in the narrow aisle. They passed without speaking. The therapist immediately intuited that his fellow passenger had suffered a deep narcissistic wound. The therapist asked himself how he could have arrived so summarily at this intuitive response to his fellow passenger. As the therapist took his seat, the woman sitting across the aisle from him looked back at the other passenger who was continuing down the aisle. She said aloud but to no one in particular, "That jerk!" The therapist recognized the term 'that jerk' as a primal judgment. The therapist's free associations to the woman's primal judgment produced a fleeting primal image of his fellow passenger jerking-off in the train bathroom. Subsequently, the therapist had ample opportunity to confirm the validity of his initial intuitive perception of his fellow passenger. He observed that his fellow passenger subsisted on a self-stroke economy. Although he was quite talkative, he spoke only to hear himself speak rather than to communicate with others. His inability or reluctance to risk relating to others and risk responding to others in an appropriate fashion became painfully obvious.

Any competent clinician observing the interactions of the gentleman in question would over a period of time have recognized that this was a very damaged and hurting individual unwilling to risk closeness.

The therapist's intuitive response to his fellow passenger took only seconds. The therapist's instantaneous and formerly unconscious primal image of the passenger as heading for the train bathroom to masturbate was recovered by his free-associations to another passenger's primal judgment of the passenger as a jerk.

The primal judgment emerges from the pictorial representation of the primal image. The socialized human being who has been taught that harboring such thoughts and images is sick, will usually have little difficulty keeping such activated images under control and unconscious.

# Cognition

The intuitive process makes use of what are sometimes defined as pre-logical cognitive processes. By pre-logical cognition I am referring to pre-scientific or pre-Aristotelian cognitive processes. Aristotelian logic states that object A is not object B and therefore object B is not object A. The Von Domarus Principle states that pre-Aristotelian logic is based on the recognition of identical predicates. In a primitive society a man may state, "I saw you talking to a man with an evil heart. The crocodile has an evil heart and stole your goat. The wildcat has an evil heart and stole your chicken. The wildcat and the crocodile are the man with the evil heart." In pre-logical or pre-Aristotelian logic, the shared predicate of an evil heart indicates that the man, the crocodile and the wildcat are the same object. A schizophrenic patient stated, "God crucified his own son Jesus. My father is crucifying me. I am Jesus."

In the evolution of mankind the pre-logical cognitive structures, as exemplified in the formulations of Von Domarus, held center-stage for a very long time (Von Domarus 1944).

Aristotelian logic and the scientific method of logical thought are fairly recent accomplishments. The infant in modern times will retrace this evolutionary path beginning with logic based on predicates. The child will subsequently supplant or abandon this form of logic as they adapt and identify with the external logic of the collective, a logic that states that Subject A is not subject B. The logic based on predicates is retained in the unconscious. If and when the modern individual's identification with the collective logic of modern society begins to falter they may regress to the pre-logic of early man. The logic of the schizophrenic only becomes comprehensible when we consider that it is a pre-Aristotelian logic. The schizophrenic suffers from an orgy of identifications with predicates. Thus efforts to comprehend the meaning of the schizophrenic's communications only on the basis of Aristotelian or scientific logic are not fruitful.

## States of the Ego

When we review the history of the evolution of fully modern cognitive processes we cannot fail to notice that the fully modern human being arrived on the scene eons before modern logic was acquired. Modern logic and cognitive processes are not the gift of either evolution or heredity. Our inheritance provides the Natural Child state of the infant's ego only with the logic of identification with predicates. The subsequent acquisition by the child of adaptation to the environment and identification with the logic of the collective may proceed only at the cost of supplanting the Natural Child's pre-Aristotelian logic. The subsequent acquisition of new states of the ego defined as Adapted Child, Adult and Parental states of the ego will be based on the identification with the logic of the collective, a logic that is based on Aristotelian logic. It is within the unconscious Natural Child state of the ego that these primitive modes of logic may be retained.

In conclusion let me restate my premise that the intuitive process in modern man begins with the unconscious and repressed archaic logic of that state of the ego identified as the Natural Child state of the ego. It is the pre-modern-logical cognitive processes retained in the unconscious of the Natural Child state of the ego that initially triggers the primal image and the subsequent intuitive process.

# 27

# The 'Natural Child' and Schizophrenia

The process of socialization of the child begins with the denial of the Natural Child's own impulses and passions as the child establishes ego identifications with the social norms of the world around him or her. It is this process of forming ego-identifications with those in their external world that allows them to exit out of the extreme narcissism that characterized the initial Natural Child state of the ego and provides the means of entering into the socialized state of the social being. The child incorporates ego-identifications not only for survival but also in response to their need for relatedness. Possibly the schizophrenic-to-be may have been less genetically endowed for the task of forming stable ego identifications than is the norm. It is also possible that the early environment of the schizophrenic presented excessive obstacles to the formation of ego identifications. At any rate it appears that in the pre-schizophrenic the ego identifications that are the basis of the socialized human being are of an 'as if' quality. They are tenuous at best and therefore are subject to decay.

When the child has difficulty identifying with their parental figures they may introject rather than identify with their parental figures.

> "The introject of the parental imago cannot immediately fuse with the rest of the ego, for the objects introduced into the ego are too magnificent, and the distance between them and the ego feeling of the child is too great."
>
> (Fenichel, 1945 pg. 104)

When their ego-identifications falter the schizophrenic is reunited with their formerly denied Natural Child state of the ego. They 'fall' into the unconscious. In the schizophrenic-to-be this Natural Child state of the ego is extremely narcissistic. Narcissism and the loss of the tenuously held ego identifications with others present the patient with the existential dilemma of extreme loneliness. They cannot relate to (identify with) others and therefore out of sheer loneliness will pay rapt attention to the hallucinated voices even though these voices are often quite abusive.

It is the loneliness of the schizophrenic that not only encourages their rapt attention to the voices of the internalized other but this loneliness also provides us with the means to 'reach' the schizophrenic. When the patient was in a florid psychotic state Rosen would direct his interventions to the patient's Natural Child state of the ego. This state of the ego is devoid of ego identifications and is therefore, at least in the non-psychotic, not directly observable. At those times when the patient is in an active psychotic state attempts to intervene with or contact Adapted Child, Adult or Active Parent states of the ego are an exercise in futility. When John Rosen (1953) would determine that the hallucinated voice was that of a maternal figure. He would say to the patient, "I am your mother." He would then hold a long conversation with the patient as their mother. When he determined that the hallucinated voice was that of God he would say, "I am God!" In this way he was able to establish contact with the patient.

The patient in a psychotic state has literally 'fallen into' the unconscious. In order to make contact with the patient in this state it is necessary to 'join' the patient in their unconscious state. Once the therapist is in contact with the patient's unconscious the patient may identify with the therapist and join him or her in conscious reality. It is the re-establishment of contact, of identification with the formerly internalized object now as an external object that allows the patient to exit out of the isolation of the psychotic state.

In a case in which I am restricted from providing more details, it was determined that the patient was listening to hallucinated voices coming from the heater vent in his room. The psychiatrist in charge of the case said, "Piece of cake! Put a mike in the vent." When the mike was installed the psychiatrist held long conversations with the patient through the mike in the heater vent. This contact established an identification with external reality that pulled the patient out of the psychotic state.

# 28

# The 'Ideal' State of the Ego

The infant newly arrived in the world does not consciously perceive a distinction between the self and the other. The sense of self is omnipotent. "I wish for the breast, the breast appears, my wish is the breast, I am the breast." (Fenichel, 1945) A conscious perception of the self as distinct and separate from the other is not initially perceived.

The evolution of the conscious perception of the self as separate from the other, even under the best of circumstances is experienced as a narcissistic wound. Such realizations deflate the child's fictitious sense of it's own omnipotence. (Mahler, 1979) The child is therefore faced with the realization of their helplessness, with the recognition that the omnipotent power may now rest entirely with the powerful mother. To again share in that omnipotent power, the child extends its ego boundary to include identification not with the parent but with the *omnipotence* of the parent. This identification with the perceived power of the parent marks the formation of a new state of the ego, a state the child will experience metaphorically as the 'ideal' state of their ego. This ideal state of the ego is quite narcissistic and delusionary. Appropriate parenting may remind the child that they are not yet a grownup and therefore they do not share in the same privileges that extend to grownups. In response to social pressures the child adapts to a new reality. This adaptation marks the birth of the Adapted Child state of the ego. This new and conscious state of the ego supplants the previous narcissistic identification with the perceived omnipotence of the parent. The supplanted Natural Child state of the ego may be defined in psychoanalytic terms as the ego ideal.

> "The ego ideal is an agency of wish fulfillment. If we pursue the further development of these hallucinatory wish fulfillments, I think we find confirmation of this assumption. When the infant has learned to distinguish between self and outer world he makes an object attachment to the breast and the mother, and he expects the mother to provide satisfaction. This object attachment is still a narcissistic one; the mother is not loved for her own sake, but as a need-satisfying object. Even the most loving and devoted mother is unable to fulfill every wish, to abolish every pain or discomfort in her child. There are always situations when the child feels disappointed, frustrated and above all powerless because he is unable to bring about a change in his painful state of displeasure. To deal with this condition, so dangerous for his self-esteem (his narcissistic equilibrium), the child develops alongside the hallucinatory wish fulfillment his comforting fantasies of grandiosity and omnipotence." (Lampl-De Groot, 1962 Pgs. 96-97)

I have had two cases in which the patient's conscious perception of reality was at all times influenced and contaminated by the Ideal Ego, the grandiosity of the unconscious Natural Child state of the ego. At all times both of these individuals exhibited an extraordinary level of narcissism and grandiosity. Both of them were apparently devoid of an Influencing Parent state of the ego. They each evidenced an unconscious wish to return to the Great Round as defined in a previous chapter. Each of them also evidenced a preoccupation (Passion) for death and destruction.

In several other cases I have encountered periodic eruptions of the formerly unconscious narcissism and delusionary grandiosity of the Ideal Ego.

## Example One

Mr. Bonser could not hold any job for long. A constant and lifelong pattern of self-sabotage encouraged the resurrection of the only partially denied narcissism and delusionary grandiosity of the Ideal Ego to alleviate his feelings of powerlessness. When he was employed as a security guard by the City Government, in protest to a national policy, Mr. Bonser flew the American Flag upside-down over a City Government building. On another occasion, Mr. Bonser attempted to subsist entirely on wild blackberries, a regime that quickly resulted in a need for hospitalization. The grandiosity of his Ideal Ego briefly assuaged feelings of inadequacy by providing him with the happy delusion that the other patients on the ward were from his own church denomination, having checked themselves into the hospital specifically for the purpose of keeping him company during his stay. Again, Mr. Bonser was employed to deliver the morning newspaper. When other personal setbacks threatened his already tenuously maintained psychic equilibrium, he again took refuge in grandiosity. He raged, "The people are not getting the news they should be getting!" He then took it upon himself to type out press releases, have copies made at the Copy Mart and insert a copy in each paper that he delivered.

Mr. Bonser then applied for a job as a psychotherapist, fully expecting to be judged as 'qualified.' He used my name with the expectation that I would provide him with a good reference.

## Example Two

As another example of the Ideal Ego providing an emergency repair job to damaged self-esteem, I present the case of Mr. Castle.

Mr. Castle was a middle-aged, late stage alcoholic living on skid road. The abuse of alcohol had effectively decommissioned the functioning of mature and realistic states of his ego. After each failure or rejection, he turned to the Ideal Ego for the sustenance of his self-esteem.

When the Forestry Department began desperately recruiting qualified people to jump out of airplanes to fight forest fires, Mr. Castle applied for a job packing parachutes. The idea of having someone in Mr. Castle's condition packing parachutes was not well received. He was summarily informed that they were only hiring smokejumpers at that time. This rejection, on top of all the other rejections, seriously threatened his narcissistic equilibrium. By the time he arrived back at the Mission where he was staying, his Ideal Ego had dealt with this dangerous threat by providing him with the comforting delusion that the Forestry Department had actually tried to recruit him as a smokejumper. He loudly proclaimed, "I got too much respect for myself to go jumping out of no airplane!"

Although the grandiosity that characterizes the Ideal Ego (Natural Child) may support self-esteem on a short-term basis, self-esteem supported entirely by the grandiosity of the Ideal Ego is highly unstable and tends to come apart and crashing down on the person, leaving them in a state of self-loathing and despair. The narcissism and grandiose self concept provided by the Ideal Ego and the subsequent 'fall from grace' when the Ideal Ego is no longer able to support such delusions is clearly evidenced in cases of affective disorders and mood swings.

## Manic States

The inappropriate and traumatic blemishing of the child's grandiosity and sense of omnipotence may abruptly 'kill' this sense of omnipotence. As a manic defense against this terrible loss, the Natural Child state of the ego may erect within the ego as it's Ideal Ego, a delusion of identification with the imago of a mythical figure invested with all the child's former grandiose perception of it's own omnipotent power. These mythical figures, identified with as the new Ideal Ego, sometimes erupt into consciousness as a manic state.

One of my patient's Ideal Ego would erupt into consciousness as an identification with Conan the Barbarian. I have also encountered the Ideal Ego as identification with Tarzan. Another Ideal Ego that made my acquaintance was Clark Kent.

## Example Three

Mr. Dominion, diagnosed as manic-depressive, was a very productive and humane individual. On occasion he would stop taking his lithium and undertake, through super human effort, to resolve various problems or situations. Although these efforts were usually successful and of a positive nature and benefit to others, they often left Mr. Dominion in a dangerous state of near or total collapse.

I asked Mr. Dominion to identify his secret identity. He said, "Sometimes I think of myself as Clark Kent in disguise." I then asked him, "What robs Superman of his strength?" He replied, "Eh! I don't know what you mean!" I was of course referring to Kryptonite. I suspected that he saw Kryptonite and lithium as synonymous. I suggested that he think about my question. The following day Mr. Dominion approached me and said, "I've been thinking about your question. Once I flushed my lithium down the toilet." Clearly, he had conceptualized lithium as synonymous with kryptonite, a substance that would rob Superman (his Ideal Ego) of his strength.

The influence of the Ideal Ego in cases of 'primary identifications' in adult men will be addressed in a subsequent chapter.

# 29

# Primary Identifications in the Adult Male

A component of the early formation of the ideal ego for both male and female children is feminine gender identification, referred to in the literature as the primary identification. Under normal circumstances the male child will resolve this gender identification by forming identifications with masculine figures, identifications that supersede the initial feminine gender identification. However, if the male child is overwhelmed by excessive and aggressive overexposure to the female genitalia, the child may be predisposed to "identify with the aggressor"(Freud, A. 1936) and retain the feminine gender identification as a component of their ideal ego.

It would appear that "identification with the aggressor" may occur only when the patient detects in the aggressor the denied passions or preoccupations of the Natural Child state of their own ego. When an individual who had been previously been successful in suppressing the sadistic passions of their own Natural Child state of the ego became an inmate of the concentration camp he quickly identified with the sadistic guards, dyed his inmate uniform black and behaved more sadistically towards fellow inmates than was the case with the actual concentration camp guards. The survival of the primary identification in adult men also requires a correlation between the Natural Child passions of the mother *and* the characterological passions of the child's Natural Child state of the ego. Without this correlation the maintenance of the delusion of femininity could not be sustained.

The survival in heterosexual men of a psychic feminine gender identification that conflicts with the reality of their actual masculine gender identity may not be in evidence much of the time. However, during periods when the man may feel vulnerable and helpless, an eruption of the feminine gender identification may occur. In my experience, the eruption of the feminine is accompanied by an extreme level of grandiosity.

The mothers of these men may have suppressed the masculinity of their sons to an extraordinary degree, but have not suppressed the masculine as a whole.

> "We shall need to be careful here, remembering that we are not discussing a suppression of the masculine as a whole, but a suppressed awareness of a specific part of it. Now we could say that inflation and masculinity are inseparable. But inflation is properly a characteristic of the phallic, and there it is creative. When the phallic is split off and inaccessible, inflation happens to that which remains; and this is the dangerous inflation which is our subject." (Wiley, 1989 pg. 14)

Mr. Buntz is a masculine appearing, middle-aged man who entered treatment with me on five separate occasions over a period of ten years. Mr. Buntz would seek treatment in an effort to avoid the consequences of his behavior, to manipulate the law or to manipulate his surviving family. His startling exhibitions of cross dressing, as well as his flagrant

financial schemes have been a source of embarrassment and legal problems for his prominent family.

During decisive periods in his childhood, the activities of Mr. Buntz
had called forth neither maternal pleasure nor approval for his accomplishments. His mother had not allowed restraints or limits to be placed
on his behavior. Mr. Buntz had been deprived of a parental influence that,
under normal parenting practices, would have provided the means to
form identifications with societies collective norms, values and restraints.
He was denied the opportunity to transform parental restraints into internal self-restraints. He had also been deprived of that optimal maternal
acceptance that would transform crude exhibitionism and grandiosity
into adaptable and useful self-esteem and self-enjoyment. He charged
through life like a loose cannon, creating havoc and damage at every turn.

Mr. Buntz terminates male therapists rather quickly. They fail to support his grandiosity. Female therapists find his efforts to fuse with them
as suffocating and frightening. They terminate Mr. Buntz rather quickly.

Mr. Buntz's inflated and delusional perception of his self and his
mother as godlike creatures is quite unrealistic. Mr. Buntz even speculated
on the possibility that he just might be a God.

The mother of Mr. Buntz developed a serious illness and died when
he was in the second grade. He attempted to negate the loss of his
mother and replace her with his teacher. He showed a Playboy center-
fold to his teacher and told her that she was beautiful just like the lady in
the picture. School authorities expressed concern that the boy was able
to access Playboy Magazine but failed to recognize the significance of
the boy's equating a picture of a naked lady with the mother/teacher. He
reported that he was allowed little time with his mother. However, she
did allow him to stay and watch while she was getting dressed prior to
going out for the evening. Also, on those occasions when his father was
out of town on business, his mother would take him into her bed. He
reported that she was sexually active with him on those occasions,
placing him between her legs.

Rubinfine, quotes Phyllis Greenacre:

"Thus, where exposure to the genital organs of another has been early and frequent, the primary incorporation of these percepts may influence identifications and create problems more than when such exposure has taken place largely in the phallic and Oedipal phases. Some degree of fusion of the image of one's own genitals with that of another individual of the same or opposite sex is universal, but the nature of the composition of the genital image varies considerably according to the actual experience of exposure."

(Rubinfine, 1957, pg. 134)

Discussing Greenacre's paper, Robert Bak underscored and enlarged on several of Greenacre's themes:

"It is in the phallic phase that partial likeness and important differences must be experienced. Elements of the fused genital image must now be rejected and separation of his image from that of the opposite sex must be accomplished."

(Rubinfine, 1957, pg. 135)

It is important, when a boy begins to separate out of a fused identification with the mother, that the mother both recognize and honor the emerging individuation of her son. The boy may then identify with the admiration of the masculine that he sees in his mother's eyes. In the case of Mr. Buntz, the mother narcissistically utilized the boy as a mirror. He identified with the mother's image of herself, which he saw mirrored in his mother's eyes.

"Every child has a legitimate narcissistic need to be
noticed, understood, taken seriously. The baby gazes at
his mother's face and finds himself therein, provided
that the mother is really looking at the unique, small,
helpless being and not projecting her own introjects
onto the child." (Miller, 1981, pg. 32)

Mr. Buntz recalled lonely hours as a child, following the death of his
mother, in which he engaged in perverse activities such as putting on
his mother's underwear.

Outward appearances could lead one to assume that the sex life of
Mr. Buntz is unremarkably heterosexual; he has been married twice and
has one child. In reality, his heterosexual activity is quite perverse in
that the sexual activity is undertaken as a means of again sexually identifying with his female partner, just as he had identified with his
mother's sexual identity under similar circumstances.

Mr. Buntz possesses an extraordinary ability to avoid prosecution for
his offenses, to cash checks for which there are insufficient funds and to
borrow money. On one occasion when he was being threatened by a
lender waving a meat cleaver and demanding repayment, Mr. Buntz
said, "You think you have troubles, I just found out I have AIDS." The
lender and his meat cleaver retreated at the prospect of contacting the
AIDS that Mr. Buntz did not have.

A symptom that may, or may not, accompany the condition we
recognize as the primary identification in adult males, is the fetish.
There is a tendency to deny or negate the complementary influence that
the fetish may exert in the formation and maintenance of the primary
identification.

# The Fetish

Fetishes are a frequently encountered and complimentary symptom that often accompanies the condition known as the primary identification in adult males.

> "Fetishism is traditionally regarded as a disorder of males, a perversion in which the ability to perform the sexual act is dependent on the concomitant awareness of an accessory and specific inanimate object. This object, the fetish, clearly represents the penis and is necessary to ward off the intense and incapacitating castration panic that the patient would otherwise suffer. To be sure, it has a bisexual meaning too, but it is the phallic significance that is serviceable in permitting intercourse or, in some instances, masturbation. According to my view of the situation, the fetishist not only endows his partner with the removable and adaptable penis, but in so doing this he can incorporate the penis himself through vision, touch, and smell, and thereby bolster his uncertain geniality."
>
> (Greenacre, 1960, pg. 191)

The survival of the illusion of the phallic woman is frequently signified by a preoccupation with odors and fecal matter. The preoccupation with smells and fecal matter indicates that fecal stools may symbolically represent a "female penis" to these individuals. (Bak, 1968)

Fetishism was a prominent feature in the psyche of Mr. Driscoll. He was a business executive who had been arrested for strolling in the park dressed in women's clothing and exhibiting a full erection. Incidents such as this had resulted in his having to relocate and start over on four separate occasions. He had entered treatment only after receiving an ultimatum from his present girlfriend. Impulses to steal women's clothing and exhibit his self in this manner arrived without warning and were apparently irresistible. It was determined that Mr. Driscoll preferred to steal soiled, rather than freshly laundered women's clothing. He was unusually sensitive to odors and remembered and recognized the odor of various perfumes even after years of non-exposure. He also passed out gum to the women that worked in his office because, as he stated, he liked the way they smelled when they chewed gum.

Mr. Adams almost lost a janitorial job for using a product on the carpet that he thought would add a little "pizzazz" to the air. The people who worked in the area complained that it made the place "smell like shit."

Each of the men referred to in this chapter, Mr. Adams, Mr. Buntz, and Mr. Driscoll, are articulate and attractive men, usually pleasant and attentive men who present an outward appearance of quiet masculinity. Nothing in their usual outward appearance or manner would indicate or prepare the observer for the sudden outbreak of grandiosity and the delusion of femininity that is a correlate of the condition known as the primary identification.

# 30

# The Birth of the Influencing Parent

In the historical past, social and economic mobility were more restricted, family life tended to be more stable than at present, and individuality was sacrificed in favor of conformity. In the present age, conformity and the rights of the society or other members of the family are often sacrificed to the rights of the individual. In the past people identified with the religion, the class, their family, their family values and the profession into which they were born. These identifications provide a secure sense of knowing who they are. (Wheelis, 1958) The birth of the Influencing Parent state of the ego requires the introjection or incorporation of the imago of parental figures.

The concerns of this chapter are the Influencing Parent state of the ego. When the imago of the parent is too magnificent and the distance between this imago and the ego feeling of the child is too great, the child is unable to identify with the imago of the parent. In such cases the child introjects the parental imago as an unconscious or preconscious Influencing Parent state of the ego. The Influencing Parent of Bernean ego state theory bears a striking resemblance to what Freud conceptualized as the 'Superego.'

Society has changed since Freud's time. Currently, family structures often are characterized by an absentee father, or by an abusive father, etc.

Robert Coles quotes a tape-recorded interview with Anna Freud conducted at Yale University in 1970:

> "In the early years of psychoanalysis we could take the Superego for granted: it was there, a big presence in the lives of our analyzed. Now, that is not always so. Now many of us are almost surprised when we meet someone who wants to be analyzed and is driven by a stern conscience that won't let go. Now it is the instincts that are, how is it put these days, all over the place, with no voice within saying no, no, or maybe I should say, a mere whisper, compared to the past [the relative authority of the conscience back then, as contrasted with the present time]." (Roth, Michael S. 1998 pg. 148)

What Freud defined as a Superego, in our present society, seems almost impotent, frequently exhibiting little or no power to curtail or suppress impulsivity and/or ill-advised behaviors. The influence and role of the psychic structure defined by Freud as the Superego seems to have been diminished; this psychic structure is often not "super." I prefer the term "Influencing Parent" as less forbidding and also less exotic than the term "Superego."

Many of the patients I have treated over the past thirty years were characterized by poor impulse control. The Influencing Parent that in Freud's time would normally have prohibited inappropriate behaviors, often in these times appears as either functionally absent or too impotent to curtail the patient's maladaptive and self-defeating behavior. Referring to this functionally absent or ineffective agency as the Superego could be misleading.

Children who are under-stimulated by the absence of positive familial interaction, yet over-stimulated by over-exposure to violence and sexuality, will have little opportunity to develop an adequate or appropriate Influencing Parent state of the ego. In the mishmash of today's society, the Influencing Parent is also mishmash. What kind of an Influencing Parent does a latchkey or MTV child get?

The unsocialized child needs an external source of values and authority. It is the process of internalizing the values of an external authority that molds and shapes the socialized state of the child. The unsocialized adult must go through a similar process to become socialized and master of their own impulses.

## Example One

A family friend was a single mother. Her teenage daughter became involved with the drug scene. The mother would find out where the drug party was, walk in and drag her daughter out by her hair. On two of those occasions, the daughter preferred charges against her mother. The police assumed a parental stance with the mother, telling her that she had no right to prevent her daughter from being with her friends. They even threatened the mother with jail time if she continued in this behavior. The mother's response to these threats was to tell the police, "Don't tell me I can't protect my daughter!"

The daughter identified with the parental stance of the police. For many years the Active Parent state of her ego indignantly proclaimed that the mother "had no right" to drag her away from her friends.

The Influencing Parent is a product of an unconscious introjection of an external reality or individual.

"That part of the ego which was altered by identification,
"the interjected parents," cannot immediately fuse with

the rest of the ego, for the objects introduced into the ego are too magnificent, and the distance between them and the ego feeling of the child is too great." (Fenichel, 1945 pg. 104)

As a result of the mother's appropriate limit setting, the daughter eventually suppressed the narcissism of her own Ideal Ego. The suppression of her own narcissism was a necessary prerequisite prior to the introjection or acquisition of an internalized imago of her mother as her own Influencing Parent state of the ego.

"Under the Parental influence, she behaved as her mother would have liked; and his includes specific maternal permissions or instigations as well as the specific maternal prohibitions generally included under the concept of Superego."

(Berne, 1966 pg. 222)

Even though the daughter's Active Parent state of the ego still protested that the mother had no right to drag her away from her friends, the newly-acquired Influencing Parent state of her own ego would thereafter figuratively drag her by her hair away from slippery places. After the daughter had grown up and had children of her own, she was finally able to say to her mother, "Thank God you dragged me out of that scene."

## Example Two

Mr. Plasil's lifestyle had been characterized by sexual polymorphism as well as drug and alcohol abuse. After his arrest for molesting a minor, he entered a program for sexual offenders. Mr. Plasil was very fortunate to receive a Deferred Prosecution rather than doing time for his offense. As part of the Deferred Prosecution agreement Mr. Plasil became active in Alcoholics Anonymous. He became very articulate in "talking the talk" but he never "walked the walk." He talked the program of AA and the Twelve Steps of the AA program, but he never worked the steps. Tenuous social control over previous predatory and perverse behaviors was established and Mr. Plasil developed a satisfactory heterosexual relationship. However, he lacked the internalization of an Influencing Parent that would prohibit deviant sexual behaviors. His attempt to control deviancy by an act of willpower faltered after several years and the relationship with his live-in girlfriend was damaged beyond repair. External deterrents derived from his relationship were aborted by the dissolution of the relationship and the Court no longer had any jurisdiction in the case of Mr. Plasil. In the absence of both internal and external deterrents Mr. Plasil was at great risk to re-offend. He then requested treatment with me. I agreed to assist and provide interpretation toward the development of insight, but only *on the condition* that Mr. Plasil would return to the AA program and this time, *work the Steps.* This he agreed to do. (AA World Press, 1952)

Working the first three Steps of the AA program diminished Mr. Plasil's narcissistic sense of omnipotence. His AA sponsor was neither an articulate nor an educated man but he rather nicely summed up the effect that working the first three Steps had on Mr. Plasil. He said, "Working the first three Steps taught him that there is a Higher Power that some call God, *and he aint it!*"

Working Steps four through nine began with making a searching and fearless moral inventory and concluded with *making amends to all those he had harmed.* This process, the actual working of the Steps, led to the incorporation of the AA program and the Twelve Steps as an Influencing Parent state of his ego.

During the period when Mr. Plasil was actively making amends to all those he had harmed, the construction crew he worked on was experiencing a good deal of dissension. At the conclusion of the day's work, Mr. Plasil said, "Okay, things aren't going right. We're going to have a meeting and find out what's going on." All the crew save one attended the meeting. It turned out that the individual who had absented his self from the meeting had been the root cause of the dissension, having frustrated and irritated every member of the crew. The next day Mr. Plasil took the man aside. Mr. Plasil explained to his co-worker what he had learned *about himself* was that he had to be rigorously honest *with himself* about how his behavior affected other people. He had learned that it was important that he make amends to each of those individuals he had harmed. He said, *"This is what I do in these situations. This is what works for me."*

The following day the man addressed by Mr. Plasil went to each member of the crew, admitted what he had done and apologized for his actions. Tension was dissolved within the crew and the work situation improved. Two days later one of the supervisors said to Mr. Plasil, "Well? Do you think you're ready to be a foreman now?" Mr. Plasil responded, "Yeah, I guess so." He has been a foreman at that company since that date.

## Intra-psychic Conflict

Up until the time that he had begun the course of treatment now under discussion Mr. Plasil had never experienced an intra-psychic conflict. His conflicts had always been with external entities. Approximately six months after his promotion to foreman, Mr. Plasil experienced his first detectable intra-psychic conflict. He was well aware that in his case the new way of life and the internalization of the ethical values of AA as his Influencing Parent would be subject to decay unless they were to receive constant reinforcement. To this end he attended no less than four AA meetings per week. On Thursday he skipped one of his regularly scheduled AA meetings to attend to some personal business. At his Friday therapy session Mr. Plasil stated, "I shouldn't have skipped the meeting. I'm glad I did because the business I took care of turned out really well *but I shouldn't have skipped the meeting.*"

Clearly in evidence was a structural (intra-psychic) conflict between the conscious ego feeling (I'm glad I did it) and the Influencing Parent (You shouldn't have skipped the meeting). Mr. Plasil's AA sponsor was a man who had been drunk for thirty years prior to being sober for the past ten years. He stated, "When I miss one of my regularly scheduled meetings I remind myself that there are at least six meetings on Saturday and another six meetings on Sunday that I can get to so *there is absolutely no reason* for me not to make up for the missed meeting."

Under no circumstances should the therapist offer impulsive, addictive patients such as Mr. Plasil even the slightest hint of support or absolution for disregarding the concerns of the newly internalized Influencing Parent state of the ego. Rigid adherence to the concerns and dictates of the newly-acquired Influencing Parent need to be encouraged, as the breaking of *even one* of the dictates of this newly-acquired state of the ego could lead to the entire structure falling apart. These very damaged individuals do not have the luxury of making a liberal decision. When the therapist recognizes that this type of patient is being strict with himself the therapist should applaud this attitude rather than encourage the patient to 'lighten up' on himself. Rigidity of character should not be discouraged in these cases. There are, of course, other patients who may need to 'lighten up' on themselves but patients such as Mr. Plasil do not fall within that category.

The clinician working with patients whose functioning had been characterized by impulsivity and a thoughtless pursuit of pleasure at all costs must prepare for an inevitable possibility. Such a patient may form an introjective identification with the therapist that is adequate to the task of curtailing impulsive and/or hurtful behaviors. However, such an identification or introjection of the imago of the therapist as the Influencing Parent may be subject to decay unless the patient is able to maintain contact with the therapist. The patient may find it necessary to maintain contact with the therapist for years or even for a lifetime.

I have been retired for a number of years. However, two of my former patients whose behavior had been characterized by polymorphous and perverse activities still find it necessary to touch base with me periodically in order to avoid relapse into old pathological patterns of behavior.

These people sometimes attach themselves to mates who eerily resemble the former therapist.

There is also the possibility that patients such as Mr. Plasil will find it necessary to maintain contact with Alcoholics Anonymous *or other ethically structured programs* for a lifetime.

# ABOUT THE AUTHOR

Ken Woods is recently retired from private practice. After a career in private practice and providing treatment within residential treatment facilities he is currently consulting, pursuing clinical research and writing. His previously published works include numerous articles pertaining to the treatment of paranoia, borderline personality disorders and the criminal personality.

# REFERENCES

Arieti, Silvano (1974) *The Interpretation of Schizophrenia*
Basic Books, Inc., New York

Bak, Robert (1968) The Phallic Woman
*Psychoanalytic Study of the Child Vol. 23: 15-36*

Bateson, G. (1956) Toward a Theory of Schizophrenia
*Behavioral Science 1: 251-264*

Berliner, B. (1947) On Some Psychodynamics of Masochism
*Psychoanalytic Quarterly, Vol. 16, 459*

Bergler, Edmund, (1949) *The Basic Neurosis.*
Grune & Stratton Inc., New York

Berne, Eric (1955) Primal Images and Primal Judgment
*Psychoanalytic Quarterly Vol. 29*

(1961) *Transactional Analysis in Psychotherapy*
Grove Press, New York

(1962) *Games People Play*
Grove Press Inc., New York

(1966) *Principles of Group Treatment*
Grove Press Inc., New York

(1969) Introduction to "Reparenting Schizophrenics"
*Transactional Analysis Bulletin 8 (31), 45-47*

(1972) *What Do You Say After You Say Hello?*
Grove Press Inc., New York

(1977) *Intuition and Ego States* TA Press, San Francisco

Broucek, Francis (1982) Shame & Its Relationship to Early Narcissistic Development
  *International Journal of Psychoanalysis Vol. 63*
Burstein, Alvin. (1970) "Chicken Little: A Game for Group Playing"
  *Transactional Analysis Bulletin, Vol. 9:33*
Bychowski, G. (1959) Some Aspects of Masochistic Involvement
  *Journal of the American Psychoanalytic Assn. Vol. 7, 248*
English, Fanita (1969) Episcript and the "Hot Potato" game
  *Transactional Analysis Bulletin Vol. 8, No. 32*
Edwards, Mary (Goulding) MSW (1968) The Two Parents.
  *Transactional Analysis Bulletin Vol. 7 No. 26 .*
Federn, Paul, (1952) *Ego Psychology and the Psychosis*
  Basic Books, New York
Fenichel, Otto (1945) *The Psychoanalytic Theory of Neurosis*
  W. W. Norton & Co., New York
Freud, Anna (1936) The Ego and the Mechanisms of Defense
  *International Universities Press, New York*
Freud, Sigmund, (1938) *The Basic Writings of Sigmund Freud*
  Random House Inc., New York
Freud, Sigmund, (1936) *The Problem of Anxiety*
  The Psychoanalytic Quarterly Press
Freud, Sigmund, (1950) *The Interpretation of Dreams*
  The Modern Library, New York
Freud, Sigmund (1952) *On Dreams*
  W. W. Norton & Co. New York
Fromm, Eric, (1973) *The Anatomy of Human Destructiveness*
  Fawcett Publications, Greenwich, Conn.
Fryer, Robin (7/17/96) *Personal Communication*
Gay, Peter (1988) *Freud: A Life for Our Times*
  W. W. Norton & C0., New York
Gear, Hill & Leido (1981) *Working through Narcissism; Treating Its Sadomasochistic Structure*
  Jason Aronson, New York

Goulding, Bob & Mary (1997) *Changing Lives through Redecision Therapy*
    Grove/Atlantic, New York

Greenacre, Phyllis, (1960) Further Notes on Fetishism
    *Psychoanalytic Study of the Child Vol. 15*

Honig, A. M. (1972) *The Awakening Nightmare*
    American Faculty Press, Rockaway, NJ

Jacobson, Edith, (1959) Depersonalization.
    *Journal of the American Psychoanalytic Association 7:581*

Jacobson, Edith, (1964) *The Self and the Object World*
    International University Press

Jaynes, Julian (1976) *The Origin of Consciousness in the Breakdown of the Bicameral Mind*
    Houghton Mifflin Co. Boston

Johns, H. D. (1974) Three Pots of Anger
    *Transactional Analysis Journal 4(3), 18-22*

Kaplan, E. B. (1976) Manifestations of Aggression in Latency and Preadolescent Girls
    *Psychoanalytic Study of the Child Vol. 31*

Khan, Masud (1964) Ego Distortion, Cumulative Trauma, and the Role of Reconstruction in the Analytic Situation
    *International Journal of Psychoanalysis*

Kinston, Warren (1983) A Theoretical Context for Shame
    *International Journal of Psychoanalysis Vol. 64*

Lampl-De Groot, Jeanne, (1965) *The Development of the Mind*
    International Universities Press, Inc.

Langs, Robert, (1985) *Workbooks for Psychotherapists, Vol. I, II & III*
    Newconcept Press, Inc., Emerson NJ

Levin, Sidney (1971) The Psychoanalysis of Shame
    *International Journal of Psychoanalysis Vol. 62*

Lower, Richard B. (1971) Depersonalization and the Masochistic Wish.
    *Psychoanalytic Quarterly 40:584*

Mahler, Margaret, (1979) *Infantile Psychosis*
    Jason Aronson, New York

Mayer, Elizabeth, (1985) Everybody must be just like Me
          *International Journal of Psychoanalysis 66:331*
Menaker, Ester, (1953) Masochism- A Defense Reaction of the Ego
          *Psychoanalytic Quarterly 22:205*
Miller, Alice, (1981) *Drama of the Gifted Child*
          Basic Books
Misel L. (1975) Stages of Group Treatment
          *Transactional Analysis Journal 5, 385-391*
Morrison, Andrew (1984) Working with Shame in Psychoanalytic Treatment
          *Journal of the Amer. Psa. Assn. Vol 32*
Mullahy, Patrick (1955) *Oedipus Myth and Complex*
          Grove Press Inc., New York
Neumann, Eric (1954) *The Origins and History of Consciousness*
          Princeton University Press
Novey, Ted 6/21/95. *Personal communication.*
Ogden, Thomas, (1982) *Projective Identification & Therapeutic Technique*
          Jason Aronson, New York
Rosen, J. (1953) *Direct Psychoanalysis*
          Grune & Stratton, New York
Rubinfine, David, (1957) Problems of Identity
          Psychoanalytic Study of the Child Vol. 6; 131-142
Samuels, Solon (1971) Games Therapists Play
          *Transactional Analysis Journal Vol. 1:1*
Schiff, J (1969) Reparenting Schizophrenics
          *Transactional Analysis Bulletin, 8(31), 47-63*
Searles, H. F. (1975) The Patient as Therapist to His Analyst.
          *Tactics and Techniques in Psychoanalytic Psychotherapy*
          *(Vol II pg. 95-151) Editor, P. L. Giovacchini*
          Jason Aronson, Inc., New York
Slipp, Samuel (1984) *Object Relations*
          Jason Aronson, Inc., New York

Spero, Moshe (1983) Shame, An Object-Relational Formulation
    *Psychoanalytic Study of the Child Vol. 39*
Thrane, Gary. (1979) Shame and the Construction of the Self
    *Annual of Psychoanalysis Vol. 7*
Von Domarus, E. (1944) "The Specific Laws of Logic in Schizophrenia."
    In Kasanin (ed.) *Language and Thought in Schizophrenia.*
    Berkeley: University of California Press
Weiner, N. (1948a) *Cybernetics, or control and communication in animal and
    machine*
    Wiley Press, New York
Weiss, Eduardo, (1950) *Principles of Psychodynamics.*
    Grune & Stratton, New York
Wheelis, Allen (1958) *The Quest For Identity*
    W. W. Norton & Co., New York
Winnicott, D. W. (1965) *The Maturational Process & the Facilitating
    Environment*
    International Universities Press.
Woods, Ken (1997) The Elitism Pattern of Defense
    *'The Script' TA Press, San Francisco*
Wiley, James, (1989) *The Phallic Quest*
    Inner City Books, Toronto, Canada

Printed in Great Britain
by Amazon